Mass with Children

This book is due for return on or befo

27 APR 2006

Celebrating Mass with Children

EDWARD MATTHEWS

CELEBRATING MASS WITH CHILDREN

A commentary on the
Directory for Masses with Children

COLLINS

Collins Liturgical Publications
187 Piccadilly, London W.1

First published 1975
© 1975 Edward Matthews

ISBN 0 00 599531 x

Nihil obstat: R. J. Cuming D.D. *Censor*
Imprimatur: David Norris
Westminster, 21 May 1975

Made and printed in Great Britain
by Wm Collins Sons and Co Ltd, Glasgow

CONTENTS

07

ABBREVIATIONS

CL   Constitution on the Liturgy, Vatican II
D   Directory for Masses with Children
GI   General Instruction on *The Roman Missal*
Letter EP Letter on Eucharistic Prayers

To Sister Clare
the Staff and children
St Vincent's Primary School
Carlisle Place, London
1965-1972

INTRODUCTION

The Directory for Masses with Children was published by the Sacred Congregation for Divine Worship on 1 November, 1973.[1] It was the fruit of years of discussion, enquiry and experiment. It is a most important document, affecting as it does the worship and liturgical education of our children, and therefore of almost the entire adult Church of the Future. To emphasise its importance (as if emphasis were needed) the Sacred Congregation has laid it down that the Directory is to be considered an official supplement to the Roman Missal itself, and publishers will include it in future editions of the Missal.

As a member of the commission which was responsible for the drawing up of the text of the Directory, I was conscious of the debt owed to those thousands of priests, teachers, liturgists and parents who for years had striven for the creation of a living liturgy for children. Now it is up to all of us who have the care of children to make their work and hopes worthwhile. This we can do only by a generous and wise application of the principles and adaptations contained in the Directory.

In the preparation and writing of this book my thanks are especially due to Father Raphael Kleiner, o.s.b., who was my mentor at the Liturgical Institute in Rome; to Mrs Suzanne Chapman for her constructive suggestions; to Mrs Mary Quinn (Patterson) for allowing me to use a set of Prayers of the Faithful which she brilliantly coaxed from her

1. See Appendix II for the full text of the *Directory for Masses with Children*.

9

class of children; to Monsignor A. Ricotti and Father M. Peluso, of Staten Island, New York, for their generous hospitality while I was writing the bulk of this commentary; and to Mrs Pauline James for her hard and accurate work in typing the manuscript (and for correcting many of my spelling mistakes!).

Chapter 1

LITURGY REFORMED

What Christianity is about

We are very lucky. Despite the radical parting of the ways at the Fall, God has never ceased trying to attract man back to him. Had we been speaking of some pagan myth, we would have had to tell the tale of an age-long battle between the gods and man, with both sides indulging in childish and colourful pranks to go one better than the other. Instead we are talking about the one, true God whose only concern is to love man and to win him back to a state of perfect love.

The Old Testament is one long tale of God's attempts to win man back and of man's sometimes good, often bad responses to his love. 'But my love for you will never leave you and my covenant of peace with you will never be shaken, says Yahweh who takes pity on you' (Isaiah 54:10). Finally, God sent his only Son - the ultimate, perfect image of his love for man.

On the face of it, that was a peculiar thing to do. Indeed, Jesus' death on the cross seemed the very height of foolishness to many people. Could God not have saved man by some easier means, by some great show of power and might which would have frightened people into submission? Yes, in one way he could have done that; he had the power to do it, but where is the love in that sort of display? And God is love. Furthermore, closely linked with the reality of God's love for man is the fact that God always respects man's nature. He deals with man as man is. After all, God created man and therefore if he were to treat man as an unthinking, unfeeling nobody then God would be untrue to himself. And that would be impossible.

There was also the problem of the infinite gap separating God and man. It is all very well making great displays of power, or sending messages by angels, but that sort of thing serves only to make the gap more obviously unbridgeable.

God's solution was breathtaking in its perfect love, its complete fittingness, its total simplicity. He sent Jesus his Son, who became a man. What was incomprehensible to finite man became flesh for man's sake. The infinite Word lived, talked, breathed, communicated like any other man. In Jesus, the gap, the chasm separating God and man was closed. In Jesus, God and man were perfectly united. In Jesus, we have the perfect expression of God's love for us.

As if that wasn't enough, Jesus finally showed just what closing the gap between God and man really meant. He, as man and God, submitted himself totally to the Father by dying on the cross. The Father showed his acceptance of his Son's self-giving by raising him from the dead and giving him the place at his right hand. Jesus passed over from death to life and opened the way for us to follow.

For us to follow. There lies the ultimate truth. Christ's ascension into heaven was not a matter of leaving man to his own devices, of telling man to be good from now on, and then sitting back to watch the result. The chasm separating God and man having been bridged in Christ it remains for all men to follow the same path - in Christ. The way to union with the Father is open to us and it is Christ's desire that we take that journey. 'Father, may they be one in us, as you are in me and I am in you' (John 17:21).

How can we follow Christ?

At first sight, there is a problem about the incarnation. If Christ became man at a particular time and place so that men might be reconciled to God, what about those of us who never had the chance to meet Christ face to face? We could not all be living two thousand years ago and resident in Israel. Yet salvation, as we have seen, can come only through the incarnate Christ.

It is not enough to say that Christ left behind some sort of 'power' or 'influence'. That is far too vague. In any case it does not match up with the principle we have just propounded. The whole point of the incarnation is that Christ works on man as man is, here and now. If the incarnation is not to be a total failure there must be, somewhere, somehow, a continuation of that incarnation. There has to be something we can turn to, and say, 'That is Christ through whom we can go to the Father.' Something we can see, hear and touch. That 'something' is the Church. 'You are Christ's body' Paul told the Corinthians, and he went out of his way to prove that he was not speaking in a metaphorical way. The fact that the Church is the living body of Christ in the world today is really the basis of Paul's theology. The result is that the entire principle of the incarnation, the coming-in-flesh, is verified. Christ still lives, not only in heaven, but here among us. The Church is the face of Christ in today's world.

Just as by listening to, talking with and touching Jesus the apostles came to know about the Father and to be united with him, so men today by using their senses can come to the same union. The Church teaches us, listens to us, can be seen by us - just as Christ did, because the Church is the body of Christ.

But there is another problem. The Church is a vast union of millions of people. Impersonal, some say. If it is the body of Christ there must be some point of contact where I can be sure that I am communicating with Christ. Had Christ come down on the earth and just stood still, saying nothing, not communicating with Peter and his friends in any way, they would have walked away in sheer boredom. Instead, as we know, he walked, talked, communicated through the senses.

The sacraments are the senses of the Mystical Body of Christ. They are the actions, the speaking of Christ for us today. And when we talk about sacraments we also mean liturgy, because there is no sacrament without liturgy (the pattern of worship that goes with the sacrament). Therefore the liturgy is part and parcel of the incarnation. We can only communicate with others by sight, sound, touch - our senses are necessarily involved in our relationships with others. There is no relationship without them. And this is also true of our relationship with Christ in the sacraments. Therefore the liturgy is essential to the incarnation of Christ for us today: through the liturgy we come into immediate contact with the living Christ. That is why the Fathers of Vatican II were able to say, 'Christ is always present in this Church, especially in her liturgical celebrations. He is present in the sacrifice of the Mass . . . in the person of his minister . . . especially under the eucharistic species. By his power he is present in the sacraments, so that when a man baptises it is really Christ himself who baptises. He is present in his word, since it is he himself who speaks when the holy scriptures are read in the church. He is present, finally, when the Church prays and sings, for he promised: "Where two or three are gathered together for my sake, there am I in the midst of them" (Matthew 18:20) (Constitution on the Liturgy 7).[1]'

The liturgy is a visible, tangible, audible thing because it is the communication of Christ with us and us with Christ.

1. The Constitution on the Liturgy is henceforth referred to by the initials CL.

Because we are human beings we need these material expressions of Christ. The liturgy is the incarnation of Christ for us today.

Changing worship

When Christ first came on this earth he did so at a particular place and time. He spoke Aramaic, behaved like other Jews of the time, wore the same kind of clothes. That was an important feature of the incarnation. Think what would have happened if he had appeared to Peter dressed in a morning suit and speaking English with an impeccable Oxford accent. That would have been a complete irrelevancy. Instead Christ lived in a way entirely in keeping with the culture of the place and time of his appearing.

If the liturgy is the incarnation of Christ for us today, it follows that Christ should use a form of communication in keeping with the culture of each particular place and time. Vatican II says, 'For the liturgy is made up of unchangeable elements divinely instituted, and elements subject to change' (CL 21). These unchangeable elements are what we might call the 'flesh' of this presentday incarnation, while the changeable elements are the 'cultural' expressions of that 'flesh'.

Language, customs, means of communication all change in time. An Englishman of the time of Chaucer would not be able to make himself understood in the streets of London today, and his clothes would lead most people to think that he had stepped out of a film set. Likewise the liturgy had become overgrown with many customs and practices whose meaning was lost in the mists of time. In many ways (though not entirely) it had ceased to be a fully efficient mode of incarnation. It was rather as if we were foreign visitors to Galilee at the time of Christ and needed an interpreter to tell us what he was saying.

We can go one step further. Christ's incarnation at one

place and one time was not only that he might contact man but also that man might contact Christ (and so, through, with and in him, the Father). Christ's coming demands man's response. That response, for it to be valid, for it to be the full expression of man as he really is, must be in the language, customs and general culture of man at a particular point in time. And that response is demanded of us today. It is demanded most of all in the liturgy because the liturgy is our highest point of contact with the incarnate Christ. We must not put on false mannerisms, false accents for our encounter with Christ in the liturgy. We must go to him as we really are. Therefore we come back again to the need for reform where the liturgy does not adequately express the people's response to Christ.

All this was seen very clearly by Vatican II. In speaking of the changeable elements in the liturgy the Council says, 'The latter not only may but ought to be changed with the passing of time if features have by chance crept in which are less harmonious with the intimate nature of the liturgy, or if existing elements have grown less functional' (CL 21).

Christ is present

Up to now we have been talking about Jesus Christ incarnate in the liturgy as if he is present now, in the Mass, just as he was when he walked around with his apostles. And without a doubt he is as really present in the Mass as he was, for instance, at Cana in Galilee. Yet there is a difference. An essential difference. Although the Mass we attend may contain a reading about his birth at Bethlehem and at the same time contains an account of the Last Supper (at the consecration), we do not meet Christ as he was at these moments in his earthly life. How could we? If we did it would mean that we would have him being born and present at his Last Supper all within half an hour. No, the point is that the

Christ whom we meet in the Mass is the risen and glorified Christ, he who now sits at the right of his Father.

Christ cannot be born again at Bethlehem, neither can he die again on Calvary. What the Mass does is to bring about that union between the Father and those offering the Mass which Christ accomplished in his death and resurrection. It is what we often call the Paschal Mystery - a handy way of expressing the fact that, by shedding his blood in sacrifice and by rising from the dead, Christ defeated sin and death and has made us a new People of God working for the setting up of the Kingdom. In the Paschal Mystery we are united with God, and that is what the Christian life is all about (Directory on Children's Masses 8).[2] The same paragraph of the Directory (D 8) goes so far as to say that the Christian life is 'unthinkable' without sharing liturgically in the Paschal Mystery. So much for those who think they can be good Catholics without the bother of attending Mass.

For that reason, Vatican II states, 'the liturgy is the summit toward which the activity of the Church is directed; at the same time it is the fount from which all her power flows' (CL 10). That is the key to our understanding of the nature of the liturgy. In another passage the Council says, 'In the liturgy the sanctification of man is manifested by signs perceptible to the senses, and is effected in a way which is proper to each of these signs; in the liturgy full public worship is performed by the Mystical Body of Jesus Christ, that is, by the Head and his members' (CL 7).

That sanctification, that making holy, is precisely the Paschal Mystery. Up to the time of the cross, God and man were united in Jesus Christ because of the incarnation. But it was only on the cross that man's complete submission was made to the Father - a submission, a sacrifice, accepted by

---

2. The Directory for Masses with Children is henceforth referred to by the initial D.

the Father in raising his Son from the dead. That passing over from slavery to freedom, from death to life, is what the liturgy of the Mass is all about. The Mass is the Paschal Mystery in signs and symbols and words.

So once again we are back at signs and symbols. They must mean something to us if they are to have their full effect. We worship as a redeemed people. It is not enough merely to be together in the same building as a collection of individuals. What we say and do should be the true worship, the true prayerful expression of a community which knows and understands and means what it is doing. Liturgy is not like a T.V. show in which a blindfolded competitor performs a certain number of what to him are pointless actions, to win a prize at the end.

Liturgy is worship in which the community can say 'yes' to each word and action because they can be seen to express that community's faith, hope and charity. And if the community cannot say its 'yes' because it cannot understand the language or the signs, then it is time for reform.

The Constitution on the Liturgy expresses the same idea with great force. '. . . holy Mother Church desires to undertake with great care a general restoration of the liturgy itself . . . both texts and rites should be drawn up so that they express more clearly the holy things which they signify. Christian people, as far as possible, should be able to understand them with ease and to take part in them fully, actively and as befits a community' (CL 21).

We have seen what the liturgy is, and why it must be reformed. Now we can move on to apply the same principles to adaptation of the liturgy, in particular for the benefit of children.

Chapter 2

ADAPTATION FOR PARTICIPATION

Reforming the liturgy is like getting on a strange bus. At first you travel along quite nicely. Suddenly, you find yourself turning into a road you have never seen before. What is more, you cannot get off because the bus just will not stop where you want it to. But after a while you are reassured, the bus rejoins the more familiar route and you reach your destination.

Many of the bishops who attended the Second Vatican Council must have been feeling something like that. Laying down the principles for the reform of the liturgy was one thing: where they led to was quite another. The principles of liturgy and of its reform are clear enough and at first reading they appear straightforward - straightforward in the sense that once a particular rite (for instance, the Mass) is reformed in its basic outlines that would appear to be that.

But the principles are not nearly so straightforward in their application. They tend to take us along all sorts of byways which many of us never expected to see. These byways have the single name 'Adaptation'. Adaptation means tailoring the liturgy to particular groups of people, places and occasions.

This follows on logically from the principles of reform which we examined in the previous chapter. There we saw that there are many changeable elements in the liturgy which assist in our encounter with Christ, here and now. Christ shows himself in the outward 'clothes' of our own time and background.

If all people at any one particular moment in time spoke the same language, had an identical education, lived in the same cultural setting, then we would need only one version of the liturgy of the Mass. However that is not so. There are different languages, different standards of education and many totally contrasting cultures. All these in the one Catholic world of today. The cultural and language differences between me and a native of, say, Uganda are almost as great as those between me and the Christians of the early Church. Yet the Ugandan and I have both been redeemed by the same Christ who is continuing the work of our redemption today whenever we celebrate the liturgy.

Just as we celebrate the Mass in a different manner from the early Christians so may we celebrate differently from Ugandans, Japanese, Frenchmen. Christ is always the same: on Calvary, in a Roman house during the persecution of Diocletian, in an African mission station, in a modern suburban church. This is guaranteed wherever the basic structure of the Mass is preserved. But the outward form of the Mass changes as Christ gives himself in the liturgy to different people, places and times.

There is nothing new in this. For a long time there was so much diversity in local Mass liturgies that you might have found a different form in each church of a particular town. Antioch, Alexandria and Rome are traditional main-stream sources of the liturgy, and within these main categories there were many subdivisions - for instance, Toledo, Braga, Milan, Lyons each had their own rite (and some still have). Even Britain gave house-room to such rites as Sarum, Lincoln, Hereford and Bangor. Admittedly the differences between these rites were often not very great, yet they existed.

Adaptation today
There is little doubt that as time goes on we will see the

growth of local liturgies once again. Already we can see the distinctive differences between a Mass celebrated with a sense of reticence in an English country town and that celebrated with exuberance and gaiety in a Southern Italian village. Different cultures: different liturgies.

At the same time the Church is pursuing a conscious policy of adaptation to particular circumstances. In 1969 an Instruction on Masses for Particular Groups was published in Rome. Though not a radical reforming document, it gave much encouragement to those who wanted a liturgy which would express the personal worship of a small community. The following year the German hierarchy was given permission to use a special Order of the Mass for deaf and dumb children. At the Melbourne Eucharistic Congress in 1973 an officially approved children's Eucharistic Prayer was used at a Mass for children.

Finally there is the Directory for Masses with Children recently published by the Congregation for Divine Worship. This is probably the best example to date of the application of liturgical principles of adaptation to a particular group within the Church.

Adaptation for children is necessary
The Directory is very much to the point when it says, 'From the beginning of the liturgical restoration it has been clear to everyone that some adaptations are necessary in these Masses' (D 20). That is a reference to the Constitution on the Sacred Liturgy which says, 'Provided that the substantial unity of the Roman rite is preserved, the revision of liturgical books should allow for legitimate variations and adaptations to different groups, regions and peoples, especially in mission lands. Where opportune, the same rule applies to the structuring of rites and the devising of rubrics' (CL 38). D 3 also refers to the same paragraph of

the Constitution. What stands out is the use of the word 'need' or 'necessary' when speaking of adaptation. It occurs in D 3, 20, 21 and 38. That is a stronger term than anything in CL 38. Why?

Participation is the key. This is what the Council said about participation:

'. . . in order that the sacred liturgy may produce its full effect, it is necessary that the faithful come to it with proper dispositions, that their thoughts match their words, and they cooperate with divine grace lest they receive it in vain . . . It is their (pastor's) duty also to ensure that the faithful take part knowingly, actively and fruitfully' (CL 11).

Knowingly, actively and fruitfully. These few words are like beacons, showing us what the reform of the liturgy is trying to do. Notice again the word 'necessary'. There is no choice in the matter, it is a necessity (we will see why later).

So in answering the question, 'Why should we adapt the Mass for children?', we can ask another in return; 'Can children participate in the Mass as it stands, knowingly, actively and fruitfully?' The answer to both questions is now obvious.

In the days before the Council, when I was a child, we often participated in the Mass by reading special prayers while the priest got on with his own, in silence. Those prayers were very pious, but rarely were they based on the actual text of the Mass. The priest got on with his job and we got on with ours. The Council has rather widened our vision of participation.

'By way of promoting active participation, the people should be encouraged to take part by means of acclamations, responses, psalmody, antiphons, and songs, as well as by actions, gestures, and bodily attitudes. And at the proper time all should observe a reverent silence' (CL 30).

Certainly prayers are still mentioned, and we often sang during Mass when we were at school. But what about actions and gestures? The prayers were simple, the hymns popular, but nothing was done to provide us with suitably childlike actions and gestures - unless you include the crowning of Our Lady's statue in May, or strewing flowers in front of the Blessed Sacrament during the Corpus Christi procession.

But then, we were children and our place was to keep quiet and behave ourselves while grown-ups got on with their prayers. Nothing wrong in that; good behaviour is important. But nothing was done to encourage child-participation. Now encouragement is important.

'... pastors of souls must promote ... active participation in the liturgy, both externally and internally. The age and condition of their people, their way of life, and degree of religious culture should be taken into account' (CL 19).

D 8 refers to this paragraph, and no wonder, since in speaking of the age and condition of the people etc., the Council seems to be thinking of special cases, such as children. (Not exclusively, however. How many liturgies for Old Age Pensioners have you seen?) Age is clearly important when considering how to encourage participation.

Participation is for children, too

'But surely not for children as well?' some people say, as if the child is bereft of all rights.

They forget one important point. It is not the age of a Catholic that matters but the fact that he is baptised.

'Mother Church earnestly desires that all the faithful be led to that full, conscious, and active participation in liturgical celebrations which is demanded by the very nature of the liturgy. Such participation . . . is their right and duty by reason of their baptism' (CL 14).

Once again, this is a section referred to by D 8. It puts the whole principle of participation in a very strong light. Not only adults, but *children* also have a right and duty to participate because they have been baptised.

Because they have a right we must do nothing to obstruct that right. The rights of children must not be ignored. More than that, children have a duty to participate.

In daily life, children have to be taught to carry out their duties. You cannot expect a child to keep his toys tidy if he is not given a cupboard or box to put them in. So with the liturgy. You cannot expect a child to fulfil his duty of active and conscious participation in the Mass if he is not given the means to carry it out.

That is why the Directory was written.

'Even in the case of children, the liturgy itself always exerts its own proper dialectic force. Yet, within programmes of catechetical, scholastic, and parochial formation, the necessary importance should be given to catechesis on the Mass. This catechesis should be directed to the child's active, conscious and authentic participation' (D 12).

'The principles of active and conscious participation are in a sense even more valid for Masses celebrated with children. Every effort should be made to increase this participation and to make it more intense' (D 22).

We will examine the role of school and parish later. The point to be emphasised here is that the Directory is a direct descendant of the Constitution on the Liturgy. It is not some optional extra in the bringing up of children. It emphasises issues which arise from the nature of liturgy and the baptism of all members of the Church.

The Church's duty

It is worth considering a little further the Church's obligation to provide children with their own adapted liturgy. The Directory is very clear on the point (D 1, 3 and 8), and in these brief references we can see the Church's consciousness of its role as teacher. Jesus Christ told the apostles to 'go out and teach all nations': today's apostles must obey that command. However things are not as easy as they were a century ago (though they were much harder for Peter, James and John). A Western world which last century was at least nominally Christian makes no such rash claim today, and consequently living in communion with Christ is very much more difficult than it was (D 1).

The Church is a mother and it is through baptism that she gives birth to her children. No true mother can abandon her children. She must look after them, feed them, teach them so that these children can grow up to maturity and play their part in the world. For the children of Mother Church that part is to live united with Christ and all the other members of the body of Christ.

The greatest sign of such unity is the gathering around the Lord's table which is really a family banquet. Everybody has a place at that banquet, and everybody must feel that he is welcome. Hence the Church's concern for the instruction and participation of children in the eucharist.

It is all very well to think great thoughts about the Church's responsibilities. But who in the Church is actually going to do the job? First, it is obviously the duty of the hierarchial authorities to provide the principles of adaptation and to grant the necessary permissions: D 1 and 3 put that idea into words. Secondly, the application of these principles is very much the task of the local community because that is where you see the Church in action (D 11). Within that community, parents (D 1 and 10), sponsors and teachers (D 11) all have their responsibilities.

Later in this book we will see how in practice these various people are to carry out their responsibilities.

Aim

Of course, there is always the chance that the Directory will be misused by the over-enthusiastic. A quick glance through the adaptations might lead some people to think that it is a list of new exercises, like a P.E. class. So read D 22, its third paragraph. External participation is no good without internal. Actions are no good without a heart fixed on God.

The aim of the Directory is expressed best of all in its final paragraph, D 55. It can be summed up: through Christ to the Father. That is of the very nature of the liturgy, as we saw in Chapter 1. In liturgy, we meet Christ, we encounter him in his Paschal Mystery; and it is only through that mystery that we are able to unite ourselves to the Father. Therefore the Directory has the highest aims: the redemption of every child through the liturgy.

D 22 expresses the same idea in terms of communion and spiritual nourishment. And if that sounds somewhat passive, as if children are being spoon-fed ('They have everything too easy nowadays'), then we ought to take D 15 into consideration. Liturgy is for living. There is no point in going to Mass if you are not going to live the life of the gospel. It is not enough for children to know all the answers to the catechism, Penny or Dutch. They must go out and be witnesses of Christ to the whole world.

All of us, of every age, must beware of falling into the trap of regarding Mass as a sort of spiritual filling-station, a place where we can 'stock up' with grace to get through another week. Of course, we do receive grace at Mass: that must never be denied. But it is a much more open-ended thing than that. If the priest were to conclude the Mass by saying, 'The Mass has only just begun. Go out and preach to all nations' then we might gain some idea of what it is all about. The Mass ought to be an explosion of Christ into the crowd.

Children have got to be part of that explosion; they have to be messengers of Christ, carrying the Good News they have received with their eyes and ears and heart in the liturgy of the Mass. Certainly if they do not do that when they are children, when they are still relatively innocent, there is little chance that they will do so when they have become worldly-wise and over-cautious.

'Special Masses spoil children'
There is one objection to special Masses for children which has been heard often in the past and no doubt will be heard often enough in the future. It is this: that once children get used to their special Mass they will eventually drift away from parish community Masses. The contrast between a children's Mass and the usual parish Sunday Mass will be so great that the parish Mass will suffer by comparison.

That of course might be an unwitting acknowledgement that the normal parish Mass is a dull affair anyway. But in any case there is little to sustain such an objection. When children are together in a school playground they play, shout, run, jump and skip just as we would expect them to do. At home, during a family meal, those same children have to learn to behave among adults, to be patient, to remain at the table, even while the adults are holding a conversation among themselves.

Children learn very quickly to live in a dual society. The world around them is dominantly adult; buildings, streets, traffic, newspapers, and so on, are all designed for adults. Only in the intimacy of home and in the school is the world scaled down and adapted to their needs. And the children appear to suffer little harm. The contrast between a children's Mass and the more usual adult Mass is merely another item in a world of contrasts which every child takes in his stride (D 2, second paragraph).

Far from creating divisions between children's and adult Masses, the Directory emphasises the principle that children's Masses should lead the children on to a better participation in the adult Sunday liturgy (D 21). It is because of this that a completely special Mass liturgy has not been composed. We are dealing with adaptation, not rebuilding. As long ago as October 1967 Cardinal Lercaro, who was then in charge of the Church's committee for liturgical reform, warned that no totally new rite would be composed for children. He said the reform was to be largely a matter of retaining the essential elements, abbreviating or omitting others, and selecting more suitable texts.

Therefore the basic structure of the Mass is always going to be the same - the liturgy of the Word and the liturgy of the eucharist with the opening and concluding rites (D 38). The contrast between children's and adult Masses will not be much greater than that between a Latin Mass and one in the vernacular, or a quiet, weekday parochial Mass and one celebrated in a great cathedral with all pomp and circumstance. To the outsider they appear as different as could be: to us who know the basic structure there is a total identity in essentials.

'*When I was a child . . .*'

It does not do violence to St Paul's words to the Corinthians if we turn them around to read: 'When I was a child I talked like a child, acted like a child and was not expected to talk and act like an adult.'

Granted what we have said above, that children must learn to adapt to many adult situations, nevertheless there is no reason why some adaptations should not be made for them. Indeed we have already seen that liturgical principles point to such adaptations as being necessary. For the very real danger is that adult forms may frighten children off the liturgy for the rest of their lives, may be spiritually harmful, as the Directory says (D 2).

Of course, that is the type of argument which conjures up the immediate retort, 'Then how is it that I and my friends never suffered such harm when we were children?' Which is the retort one expects from the 30% of our Catholic population which still attends Mass regularly. What, though, about the 60% who have lapsed or rejected the Church?

No one is going to claim that children's Masses are the answer to the Church's problems. Yet we are living in a world different today from that of our own parents. Discipline is regarded in a different light (regrettably, some say) and it is no longer possible to force children to do things just because of somebody's unexplained command - 'Because I say so!' Modern educational methods rely heavily upon learning by experience, rather than learning by rote, and if the Church, especially in the liturgy, does not make use of the discoveries of educational science then we may find ourselves in an even worse situation than we are.

The liturgy is a school. Or, as the Council puts it in rather more formal language, 'it contains abundant instruction for the faithful' (CL 33). Twice the Directory refers to this - D 2 and D 12, but points out (in D 2) that the adult forms of word and gesture make the educative value of the liturgy almost ineffective for children. Is there any reason why children should be excluded from one of the effects of the liturgy?

Are children lesser citizens with no rights? No. They are as much baptised as is the Pope, or you and I, and therefore have as much right to participation in, and help from, the liturgy as any grown-up.

What age of children is the Directory talking about?
Children grow and develop at a great rate. Between the ages of 2 and 15 there can be as many as eight distinct stages of growth. Therefore it is not possible to devise a rite of the Mass which will be suitable for all of them. The Directory sensibly confines itself to children who have not yet, or have only recently, made their first Communion (D 1) - to those who have not yet reached the stage of 'pre-adolescence'.

For normal practical purposes this means that the Directory is aimed at children in the 5-11 age group. Even within that range there are several stages of growth, but the adaptations contained in the Directory can easily cope with that problem.

That the Directory should confine itself to this one group of children should cause no surprise. It is precisely at this age that children are most receptive and impressionable, and they often have a religious sense which puts many of us 'professionals' in the shade. These are the sort of children who are going to benefit most from an adapted liturgy. When they enter their teens they will have an experiential knowledge of the Mass which will carry them through to a full participation in adult liturgies. By the time a child reaches secondary education he is becoming more capable of understanding some of the adult words and gestures of the Mass, and in any case the adaptations already built into the Roman Missal are such that it is relatively easy to adapt it for teenagers.

Don't throw this book away if your children are not in the 5-11 age group. The Directory has got something for all ages. Precisely because it is based on liturgical principles, the Directory can teach the entire community what adaptation really means. Until now the Anglo-Saxon and Celtic forms of Catholicism have prevented us from making that freer use of the Roman Missal which its compilers envisaged. Somehow many of us have been hung up on the notion that if it is not printed in the book then it cannot be done. For instance, that phrase 'in these or similar words', which occurs so often in the Missal, is almost a dead letter in most of our parishes. And dead letters make lifeless liturgy.

The Directory for Masses with Children is an indication of the spirit of celebration which the Church wants in its liturgy. A few pages ago we went to some pains to demonstrate that children deserve as much consideration as adults in the liturgy. We can turn that round the other way: adults deserve as much consideration as children. It is the experience of many priests (the present writer included) that good children's celebrations lead to better adult celebrations. In some way, involvement in children's liturgy brings us to a deeper understanding of the meaning of the liturgy so that the whole of our liturgical practice becomes more meaningful.

There is another point. The Directory bases itself on already existing principles. It does not make new ones. Therefore it should follow that, given special circumstances, some of the adaptations, or variations of them, can be applied to adult celebrations. An example: the omission of the prayers between the Our Father and the invitation to communion. There could well be a reason for doing that at, say, a house Mass for a sick person. The *principle* of adaptation is the same for young and old, healthy and ill.

However there is the question of authority. We cannot take the law into our own hands. The liturgy is for creating unity, not destroying it. Permission from a bishop would presumably be required, but with the valid precedent set by this Directory there appear to be many possibilities of adaptation for much older people, particularly for those in special groups.

Chapter 3

EDUCATION FOR WORSHIP

'Experience is the best teacher.' People have been saying that for generations, possibly for centuries. Doing a thing is nearly always more instructive than reading about it in a book. For example, no amount of book-learning about how to drive a car can take the place of sitting behind the steering wheel with an instructor by your side. That is not to say that the books are to be thrown out of the window as useless. Refusing to learn the theory is as big a drawback as knowing all the theory and having no practical experience.

Strangely, the truth that experience is the best teacher has become generally accepted within the world of primary education only within the last twenty years or so. Many of us still retain the traditional concept of the schoolteacher as someone who made us learn things by rote. That form of learning is still necessary as a part of the educational process: but it is only a part. Parents are sometimes disturbed when their children seem to be learning nothing at school, cannot answer simple questions, and apparently spend the school day 'painting and playing'. What they find hard to understand is that carefully directed play and apparently 'free' activities are helping the child in a very crucial stage of his development.

The same applies to liturgy. It is a lived experience. If it were not then there would be no need for us to go to Mass on Sundays - we could read about it in our books instead. Therefore the best liturgical education is liturgy itself - active worship. But just as a learner-driver is only gradually taught the mysteries of the gear change, so a child cannot be expected to play a full part in the Mass without first experiencing forms of liturgy suited to his development.

Family as teacher

Who is going to do the teaching? The most important teacher is the family in which the child is brought up. That this is so in the field of religious education hardly needs proof; no amount of intensive religious instruction at school will make a practising Catholic of a child from a completely lapsed family. (Hence the problem of the acceptance or non-acceptance into Catholic schools of children from lapsed families.) The family home is the best of classrooms.

Such a notion is not new. It comes from the nature of the family. That is why Vatican II's Declaration on Christian Education was able to say, 'Since parents have conferred life on their children, they have a most solemn obligation to educate their offspring. Hence, parents must be acknowledged as the first and foremost educators of their children' (n 3). Important as the school may be, it can never take the place of the home, and professional teachers are but the helpers of the principal teachers - the parents. This truth flows from the nature of parenthood.

To be a parent it is necessary not only to give life to a new human being, but also to do everything possible to make that new life more fully human. Becoming human starts with birth: it does not end there.

Christian parents give life to their child twice. Once at the human level and once at the divine. They give physical birth to a new child and then take that child to the baptismal font where he is born again of water and the Holy Spirit. Thus arises a dual responsibility of education. Just as physical birth demands the follow-up of human education, so spiritual re-birth into the life of Christ requires a process of education to be conducted by those who made that re-birth possible - the parents (cf D 10).

The Declaration on Christian Education links the two aspects of education so closely that they are complementary. Education for entry into the civic community and for entry into the People of God is part and parcel of the same process. It is important to realise this because all too often some parents try to throw all their educational responsibilities upon the shoulders of the teachers in the Catholic school. At the same time, they are occasionally encouraged in this by teachers and priests, who act as if parents sign away such responsibilities the moment the child goes to school for the first time.

Living sacramental love
Quite apart from the fact of having given life, parents have one unbeatable advantage over the best of schools in the education of their children. Parent and child live a life of love sealed by the sacrament of marriage. That is something no professional teacher or devoted priest can match.

Education is for loving: loving God, and my neighbour as myself. What better way of learning about that love than by seeing and experiencing it in action? For the true Christian spirit is the living together of all people in union with Christ, and the Christian family is this in miniature. It is the microcosm of the truly Christian society, the Kingdom of God. St Paul bases his teaching about marriage upon this truth. He concludes his famous passage about marriage in Ephesians by stating, 'This mystery is a profound one, and I am saying that it refers to Christ and the Church' (5:32).

Sacraments are signs, and marriage is a sacrament because it is a sign of the union of Christ and his Church. The Christian child is born into a sacramental life. He is brought up in it. He lives it. So we are back where this chapter started: experience is the best teacher.

The living experience a child receives in his family is not that of a perfect society. Families have their ups and downs, their good times and their bad. But what he witnesses is the life of love of two people, his mother and father; a life in which he has an important part to play since he is a product of that love. He will see and enjoy the times of happiness, suffer in times of difficulty, withstand the times of boredom. And all the while the child is experiencing, mostly in an unconscious manner, the virtues of tolerance, mutual consideration, self-sacrifice, forgiveness, shared joy - all those virtues which go to make up a happy yet human marriage.

Family and liturgy
It is therefore no surprise to discover that the Directory for Masses with Children makes special mention of the role which parents can (and should) play in the liturgical education of their children (D 10). The reasons we have seen: the methods are equally interesting.

Liturgy is the divine acting in a human manner. Human gestures, words and symbols are used to communicate a spiritual reality. The first task of parents is to teach their children the meaning of the ordinary gestures and signs which people use among themselves. Normally we do not think of the connection between our everyday gestures and those of the liturgy, but the connection is real. In fact, we can go so far as to say that the child who has not been brought up to understand and appreciate the common courtesies of everyday life will be unable to understand most of the basic liturgical gestures and concepts of the Mass.

Examples are obvious: saying 'hello' to a visitor at one's home (the Greeting and its response at the beginning of

Mass); saying 'sorry' for having done something wrong at home or at school (the Penitential Rite); learning to give way to others and not preferring oneself (assembly of the community); listening to what others have to say (Liturgy of the Word); saying 'thank you' (Liturgy of the Eucharist i.e. of Thanksgiving); sharing formal meals (Communion); celebrating special occasions such as birthdays (celebration of church feasts) (cf D 9 and 10).

Remember this is not the training of a child to 'behave properly' at Mass, in the sense that the child must keep quiet and not disturb the adults. We are speaking of something far deeper. We are speaking of training for worship.

These human values, as the Directory calls them, illustrate very clearly the 'incarnational' aspect of the liturgy. Christ becomes present under the appearances of the normal world. Furthermore the dual purpose of these values (human-liturgical) shows clearly how liturgy and life are not two distinct never-to-be-confused realities. Liturgy is the sanctification of life. The wedding of divine and human.

Naturally, no parent will teach a child these human values simply because they help the celebration of the liturgy. But it may happen that in individual cases children are not receiving this basic upbringing in human and Christian living. What then?

We have said that children from lapsed families usually do not grow up believers no matter what efforts are made by the school which the children attend. But that does not mean that the children are to be abandoned to their fate. Many a family has returned to the practice of its religion as the result of work done by the school for the child. Catechism classes and baptismal sponsors can also have the same effect (cf D 9, 10 and 11).

Not only *can* they have the same effect: they *must*. At baptism it was not only the child's family which accepted certain responsibilities for his religious upbringing. That child was baptised into a community: he became a member of the Body of Christ. The other members, for the sake of the child and for the sake of the health of the Body, have a duty before God to help in the education of all baptised children.

With this principle we are at the very heart of the raison d'être of our Catholic schools. This is not the place to discuss the subject in detail, but there is one truth that every Catholic priest, parent, teacher and catechist must understand. It is this: the Catholic education of children is not an optional service by the local parish. It is an obligation, a duty. Every time we accept a baby for baptism we are accepting responsibility for that child. Who knows what we will have to answer for at the Day of Judgement when it comes to the comparison of baptisms performed and subsequent duties fulfilled? It is easy to bestow a sacrament. Not so easy to follow it up.

Moreover the follow-up must include a liturgical formation, not merely a dogmatic exposition of what the Mass means, important as that may be. In other words, the whole community has the responsibility to help its children participate in the Mass, consciously, actively and fruitfully. For that reason the Directory for Masses with Children must be seen as a document for the entire Church. It is not a specialist's tool, designed solely for the use of teachers and school chaplains.

Prayer in the home

Empty gestures are useless, even harmful. What gives liturgical gestures their meaning is the prayer that goes with them. That starts in the home too.

Unfortunately prayer in the home has taken a big knock in recent years. The days of regular family prayer appear to be over. Indeed a feeling of embarrassment comes over the parent when the subject of prayer crops up. They are embarrassed to pray, and embarrassed to talk about it.

On the other hand, there are some hopeful signs. Prayer groups and the charismatic movement are beginning to make themselves felt in some quarters. These groups are growing in number and influence. Who knows but that we are witnessing the beginnings of a return to a life of the laity solidly based upon liturgy and shared prayer?

Families need prayer: families need to pray together. God is the very source of that life which parents and children share - both physical and spiritual. Ignore God and we ignore life itself. Parents have cooperated with God in creating new life, and they obeyed God's will by making that new life a redeemed life in the waters of baptism. Therefore they have an obligation to reveal to their children the life-giving fatherhood of God - and that can come only through prayer (cf D 10).

The prayer of the family, as family, should be the most natural thing in the world. It is a turning to God to acknowledge total dependence. It is the point of recognition that the family is united in Christ; that all fatherhood on earth takes its title from the fatherhood of God.

Prayer is an indispensable ingredient of liturgy. Without prayer liturgy is a sham, an empty pantomime. So praying together is not merely an end in itself: it is a preparation for worship.

We can go further than that. Praying together *is* worship. When a family gets together to pray, there is Christ in the midst of them (cf Matthew 18:20). The praying family is the Church at that moment. The family is a praying community.

That point is important in the formation of the child's attitude to praying and to church-going. It can help a child

39

realise (gradually, of course) that praying is not a specifically 'churchy' activity: a peculiar habit practised in a peculiar building. And it can also teach the child that what takes place in church can also be done at home. Religion does not begin and end at the doors of the parish church.

Ultimately there is nothing to prevent a child understanding that the reason why he goes to church is so that he can pray *with other people*. Just as his family is a praying community so his family is part of a larger praying community - a coming-together of many other small praying communities. In the same way that each child's contribution to the family prayer is important and indispensable, so the contribution of each family to the prayer of the local community is important and indispensable to the building up of the family of God (cf D 16).

There are also advantages from the behavioural point of view. A spontaneous and easy-going atmosphere will naturally be more suitable to family prayer. Nevertheless a certain formality can sometimes be introduced which demands the attention and good conduct of the child. Once this principle is established in the child's mind it should not be too difficult to demand of him a certain level of good behaviour when he attends Mass at the local church. This is not a question of 'slapping down' but of training the child at home to recognise different moods of prayer - solemn, joyful, sorrowful, silent, vocal, sung, read.

Never be too surprised at the naughtiness of children in church. Sometimes parents appear to ignore the comfort of other worshippers and make no attempt to control their offspring. But it is important to appreciate the strange situation most children encounter when they go to Mass. Even apart from the large number of adults, it is quite unlike anything they encounter elsewhere. Without preparation they are almost bound to react in a noisy, restive manner.

Home liturgy and frequent family prayer is the best preparation.

How to pray in the home

Theory is one thing: practice another. Most Catholic parents recognise the need for family prayer, but how to set about it is the problem. The obvious starting-point is morning and night prayer, and of the two, night prayer normally receives some sort of attention from the majority of families.

The pedigree of morning and night prayer is unimpeachable. It corresponds to the Church's own official prayer of Lauds and Vespers. What better way to start the day than by dedicating it to God at the very outset? What better way of concluding it, than by thanking God for his blessing and asking his forgiveness for missed opportunities?

But there is still the problem of the 'how'. Here some readers may be a little puzzled. 'Surely', they will say, 'there is little difficulty? We always make sure our children say their prayers.' It is in the 'we make sure' that the mistake lies.

How many parents pray *with* their children? How many do that every day, as a matter of course? All too often a mother slips into the habit of folding up clothes, putting away toys and generally tidying up the bedroom while little Johnny and Mary stumble through their routine at the side of the bed. (With a few parental promptings when they go wrong.) Even worse is the guided tour of children's night prayers which some parents insist on inflicting upon visitors. A crowd of tittering and embarrassed onlookers make poor Johnny look like a performing animal in a circus act.

If you want your child to pray you must get down on your knees with him. Only in that way will he learn the worth of what he is doing. Otherwise he will associate prayer with childhood. 'Grown-ups don't pray.'

Praying together with his family, the child will begin to experience the practice of community prayer: he is only one step away from participation in the Mass. He is gathering, albeit in a small way, the experience of what it means to be a member of the Church.

Although the words of these family prayers will be largely at the level of the understanding of the child yet the parents should not be wholly condescending. They should pray their own prayers out loud so that the children, though not understanding, might hear them. In this way the child will see that prayer means something to adults, that such great and powerful figures as his mother and father need to turn to God for help, forgiveness, in thanksgiving. A further result of this experience will be that the child gradually learns to expand the scope of his own prayer and learns to pray for the needs of other people, who perhaps do not have any direct contact with him.

The benefits are reciprocal. There is much we can learn from the simplicity and directness of a child's prayer.

The ideal is for the entire family to gather together for prayer every evening. In this way a true community spirit is engendered. There are all sorts of difficulties to this, the principal one being that of getting everybody together at the same time. But even if the entire family can be assembled only once or twice each week, something of worth will be accomplished.

Meanwhile we must not forget the enormous benefits of silent, private prayer (cf D 10). What we are educating our children to is a loving relationship with a God who has proved, and continues to prove, his love for us. It is a personal as well as a community love. Each one must make his own approach to God. Prayer in common will only be as good as the quality of the private prayer of the individual members of the community. But the very young child will more easily come to the experience of private prayer through the previous experience of praying with others.

This still leaves us with the question of what children should pray about - a question more easily answered by the parents themselves. The main point is that we should avoid overmuch stress on prayer of asking - prayer of petition. There is many an adult who knows only how to ask God for something. ('I always pray to God when I am in trouble.')

We should teach our children to praise God for his great goodness; and for the young child that means God's goodness today, in particular ways. There is a need to tell God how sorry we are for not matching up to his love. And God must be thanked for his love.

Much of this prayer can and ought to be practised, not only at special times of the day, but whenever the occasion arises. Thus a child's wonder and delight at the antics of a kitten can be quickly summed up in a prayer with his mother. Only a couple of seconds are needed, half a dozen simple words and God is consciously seen as part of the pleasure. At pre-school age and for some time after, children are very susceptible to this form of prayer. They accept most easily the notion of a loving God who guides all things, even though their concept of God is rather primitive.

Home liturgy

Prayer is not just words. It can also be action, movement. No young child can put up with conversation for long; he has got to do things, not just talk about them. With this facility he is half-way to the liturgy because that activity of the Church is never words only. Liturgy is a mixture of words, movement, signs and silence. So why not have liturgy at home, not only as a preparation for going to Mass, but also as real family prayer? (D 13 and 14).

It is not very difficult to make up simple liturgies to celebrate the seasons of the year, to ask God's protection before a holiday journey, to celebrate a birthday, to beg healing for a sick relative. Prayers, home-made models, processions around the house, the use of candles and water, and many other things besides - all these can be used by the most ordinary of families. This writer knew a family which composed its own Litany of the Saints and sang it while walking in procession around the garden in imitation of the Church's Rogation procession. A litany which includes the patron saints of parents and children, as well as special intentions, is an easy prayer to compose.

If these ideas of home liturgy seem unreal to some readers, we need only recall the 'altars', family rosary and dedication of the home to the Sacred Heart in days not so long ago to remind ourselves that these are not new ideas at all. This is not the place to go into this subject in any more detail, but parents are recommended to read the books of Oliver and Ianthe Pratt in which they give very many practical examples of home liturgies (e.g. *Let Liturgy Live*, Sheed and Ward, 1973).

'What else must we teach our children?'

Once parents get down to a life of prayer and home liturgies there is no end to the possibilities. We have already seen that parents have the primary obligation to bring up their children in the faith. Questions about that faith are bound to crop up in a family that prays and worships together. How many parents feel competent to answer these questions? Very few.

The formal religious education of most of the laity ceased

the day they left school. The knowledge of their faith has usually failed to keep step with their increasing knowledge of their job, of people, of life. They have children's answers to grown-up problems. This is not their fault. Nevertheless this must be one of the commonest (though unconscious) grounds for the drift away from the Church. Like St Paul, such people reject childish ways and if there are no adult ways to take their place they gradually disappear from our churches.

What is to be done for the parents who want to do the best for their children? First, there must be a reform of the Church's approach to the instruction of the adult laity. This reform must start in the pulpit, because so much that is said there is either above the heads of the listeners, or ill-prepared, or irrelevant. In other words, education starts with the clergy. But that is the long-term measure. There is something we can do for parents now.

Every Catholic primary school should assume the responsibility of educating parents as well as children. With the school staff available and helped by the local clergy, or representatives of the diocesan catechetical team, courses can be held to take parents on a few steps, further away from their 'school-leaver' level of religious knowledge. The easiest way of doing this is by linking the course with the sacraments for which their children are currently preparing (cf D 10).

By taking the line, 'This is what we are teaching your children', a door can be opened to a renewed interest in the faith, and to cooperation in the preparation of the children. Such a course must be short and snappy. A talk by a teacher on what and how the children are being taught, followed by some adult applications by another speaker, perhaps a priest. If well-prepared, this often leads to requests for further information either in the same format, or in smaller groups. Simple, straightforward facts about the faith have the power of provoking great interest.

To crown such a course, what better than a non-sacramental liturgy planned and performed by the children (D 10)? With suitable gaps for their participation, most of the grown-ups would most likely experience something entirely new in their religious lives.

Non-sacramental liturgies have the great advantage of being adaptable as and when required. For example, a bible service, based upon the children's renewal of baptismal vows (in a darkened room with candles lighted from the Paschal candle), followed by the parents' renewal of their promise to bring their children up in the practice of the faith. Or maybe a short service on the theme of Sharing Life, ending with some of the children handing around (sharing out) the tea and biscuits.

This is also a good opportunity for making contact with lapsed parents. Experience shows that nearly everybody will attend a function to discuss their children. Apart from the truths of the faith which can be explained, the non-sacramental liturgy is a step towards full reconciliation at the altar rail. Many lapsed parents have used such occasions to talk privately with the priest, resulting in a return to the sacraments. It is surprising how many people give up the practice of their religion for reasons which owe more to lack of knowledge than to lack of faith. The local school can provide the opportunity for putting them right.

This applies equally to the situation in which children do not attend Catholic schools. Voluntary catechists, trained for the work, can do much for the Church not only in teaching the children, but also by aiming their sights at the parents.

Some experts believe that the catechist should spend most of his time with the parents, not the children. The writer was provided with an example of this in the poor district of a big city where most of the grown-ups had lapsed. It was made clear to the hundred and twelve applicants for First Communion that they would be admitted to the sacrament only if their parents conducted the instruction.

After much door-knocking and arguing, the catechetical team succeeded. A hundred and ten out of the hundred and twelve parents attended a course of instruction which they then handed on to their own children. The result was that whole families were renewed in the knowledge and practice of their faith.

Could this be the pattern of religious education in the future? Is this the answer to the shortage of places in Catholic schools? Can we see in the future a complete renewal of our Catholic laity's understanding of the faith? The answers to these questions depend upon the faith and energy of teachers and priests today.

The job of the schoolteacher
So far we have affirmed two principles. First, that parents have the prime responsibility for the religious and secular education of their children. Second, that the entire community has a responsibility of some kind to every child baptised in its midst (D 11).

As one would expect, Vatican II's Declaration on Christian Education has much to say on this subject. Of teachers it says, 'Above all, let them perform their services as partners of the parents' (n 8). Partnership is a good description of the role of parent and teacher.

The Directory on Children's Masses (D 11) underlines three ways in which all members of the community help its children - Witness, Charity, Celebration. Briefly, let us take a look at how these three qualities can be applied to the Catholic teacher.

47

Witness: the teacher is not just a dispenser of information. She must be someone to whom the life, death and resurrection of Christ are all-important facts of life. Faith has to be lived, not just learned. The spirit of the teacher does much more for the faith of the children in her care than all the facts and figures of dogmatic definitions.

Not that dogma is unimportant. Far from it. But if it is to be lived by the children (and there is no point if it is not), then they must see it alive in their teacher. She does not teach in class the Highway Code and then step off the pavement in front of a bus.

Witness is not something easily defined or described. You cannot pin it down like a desiccated butterfly. It is a spirit animating the teacher which children instinctively recognise, although they may not be conscious of it. But the children should be able to sense that 'Our teacher practises what she preaches.'

Being a witness is not easy. It demands a teacher who is concerned for the world, who is concerned for people and the problems facing them. She must be someone who is totally convinced that the message of Christ is a message for all men at all times.

Witness to the gospel is not a nine to five job. It is not the look of grim determination assumed on stepping out of the Staff Room after a tea-break.

Doubts will come, sometimes even despair. But it is the sign of true witness that the teacher should keep going even in the face of the gravest difficulties - difficulties of faith, difficulties from the Church's own representatives, difficulties from apparent lack of success, difficulties from a world increasingly irreligious.

Underpinning witness is prayer. You cannot proclaim the gospel without at the same time being in contact with its source - Christ. Prayer is the life-blood of Christian teaching and without it our words are lifeless. Basically it is living in Christ in such a way that we can approach him in prayer with an easy familiarity. There are times when a more informal approach to prayer is required. The formality is present in the liturgy and in the many occasions of school prayer. The informality is more personal and, considering the exhausting nature of a teacher's work, particularly in primary education, is more suited to the out-of-school life of the average teacher.

Charity: Catholic schools above all demand the fulfilment of the commandment, 'Love thy neighbour as thyself.' Staffs should be motivated by a genuine love of the children they teach. Children are not just a 'job', a way of earning a salary (there are easier ways, in any case). Teacher and child are united in Christ and help form the one Body of Christ. So also teachers among themselves. Staff-room feuds, petty dislikes, lack of cooperation should have no place in a school founded on Christian principles. A Catholic school should be the Church in miniature where all things are done in, with and through Christ.

Celebration: means putting into symbolic form all that is learnt in school and making of it an act of worship to God. Liturgical celebration transforms the most mundane aspects of teaching and learning into a way of praising God. The liturgical seasons, feasts of our Lord, our Lady and the saints are so much theory until they are put into liturgical form. Celebrated, they begin to live. There is no dogma of the Church which cannot be celebrated in the liturgy.

The same applies to the secular subjects taught in school. They should be celebrated periodically to show that all things come from God and must return to him. In Christ all things have been created, and in him they have been redeemed. Progress in reading, the history of the kings and queens of England, the use of weights and measures - these

are only some of the items that can be prayed about, celebrated in a liturgy. (More of this in Chapter 6.) If it cannot
be celebrated, it cannot be taught.

These celebrations are an ideal opportunity for initiating
children into the mysterious gestures and signs of the Mass
liturgy (D 13). A start could be made by calling the children
together when some discovery has been made (for example
a plant coming into flower), and pausing for a brief,
spontaneous prayer. Carefully planned liturgies mark the
completion of a project which has occupied the class for a long
time. As the children become used to this practice they
are introduced to more and more liturgical gestures and
attitudes. Their introduction to the Mass will therefore be
gradual and not a sudden plunge into a sea of confusing
gestures and words.

The principal ingredient of these liturgies must be prayer,
whether composed by the children or by the teacher,
spontaneous or prepared. On a par with prayer is the Word,
the bible (D 14). It is only through scripture that we know
we can pray and know our prayer will be heard. It is God's
Word, the voice of God in human language, speaking to us.
What better teacher than him?

When scripture is used in school, it runs the risk of being
regarded as a source of 'edifying' stories and handy phrases
used to prove a point. Its use in a liturgical setting is a way
of showing that it is something living, something which
must be listened to just as we would listen to God himself.
The way the book is honoured, the solemnity with which
the reading is done, serve to make the children aware of the
treasure at their disposal.

Finding suitable passages can be a problem for teachers.
Fortunately there are now many simplified versions of the
bible for children set out in a way that is easy and attractive to read. It is also a good idea to use the scriptural

passages from Mass theme books; these passages are usually pre-selected for a theme which children can easily understand.

It would be a mistake to think of these school-room liturgies merely as a preparation for an understanding of the Mass. They have an importance in their own right. The Mass liturgy is not the only one worth celebrating. Moods and needs of children differ: such moods and needs may sometimes be better served by a non-eucharistic liturgy (D 27). The Mass has a certain air of formality, and its basic structure is well-delineated: this may not be suitable for the spontaneity and gestures which a teacher judges necessary for particular occasions. For example, to thank God for the fruits of the earth a celebration in the local park may be more effective than a Mass in the church. The priest is often unavailable for Mass.

The Mass could possibly come as the culmination of a whole series of non-eucharistic celebrations (D 27). This has the advantage of placing the preparation for the Mass in a setting of prayer and celebration so that the step from non-eucharistic to eucharistic celebration is a natural one. The best ideas from the informal liturgies may be used for the culminating Mass.

Or we can go in the other direction: the Mass as source of a subsequent series of minor liturgies. The various ideas present in the celebration of the Mass are in this instance separated out and provide material for individual acts of worship either in classroom or assembly hall.

However and whatever is done one dominant principle prevails. The Catholic teacher is a leader of worship. She is someone who is deeply aware of the relationship of all things in Christ and can help the children to express this in word and gesture. The Catholic school will thus become a worshipping community.

This chapter can best be summarised thus: the celebration of Mass by children will depend for its success not so much upon what is done or not done at that Mass, as upon the ability of parents and teachers to show children that prayer and worship are a way of life and a part of life.

Chapter 4

WHAT CHILDREN NEED TO KNOW ABOUT THE MASS

There is a moment of truth which all teachers fear. A project has just been completed; the children have been involved in it step by step, and all looks rosy until the teacher asks, 'Now why did we do that? What was it all about?' The answer: silence. Blank incomprehension.

It is not enough that children should do a thing well: they should also know why they are doing it, what it is all about. In the last chapter we came to the conclusion that experience is a good way of learning. But it is not the only way. In this chapter we must take a look at the theory, the theology a child ought to know about the Mass.

Scores of books and articles have been written about what children should know about the Mass and how it should be taught to them. It is not within our scope to add to all that writing. We will confine ourselves here to the rather general outlines found in the Directory for Masses with Children. A more detailed treatment can be found in the General Catechetical Directory, though even that is still rather brief. The fact is that the Church is well aware of the vast differences in age, background and competence among children, which makes it well nigh impossible to lay down rigid rules about what should, or should not, be taught. What is certain is that some dogma is essential. Children are not animals: they have minds, and these minds need to be fed. Pure experience needs to be balanced and supported by the whys and wherefores. On the other hand, children are not theologians and we should recognise that there is a limit to the amount of dogma they can take. And this is not merely a question of discovering the right teaching method, although some people (usually non-teachers) appear to assume that any and all dogmas can be learnt by a child of ten as long as you set about it in the right way. All dogma is for living – to help us know, love and serve God as Christ would have us do. If particular dogmas have no immediate relevance for a child of ten we may well be wasting our time teaching them. There is a right time for everything.

The liturgy teaches (D 2 and D 12)
The liturgy teaches because in the liturgy is present the greatest of all teachers – Christ. The Constitution on the Liturgy (CL 33) uses this fine phrase: 'For in the liturgy God speaks to his people and Christ is still proclaiming his gospel.' When we participate at Mass we are listening to the teaching voice of Christ. Christ, our Teacher, is really present at the Mass in the community, in the minister, in the Word and in the eucharistic species.

The fact that the liturgy teaches means that we still have much to learn. This ought to be some consolation to those priests and teachers who think their young charges do not know enough about the Mass. You don't need the knowledge of an Aquinas to make your First Communion. Surely even St Thomas learnt more by celebrating the Mass. Weak faith, strong faith, all kinds of faith are nourished by the Mass (cf CL 33). The Mass is not a reward for those who can memorise, parrot-fashion, certain wordy facts about the faith. It is for the weak, the struggler, the learner, as well as for the saint and theologian.

We must use the Mass as a teaching instrument. Not that the Mass is merely another educational tool: far from it. Of its nature, the Mass is made up of signs and symbols which tell us of realities which we would not otherwise know about. Teaching children about the Mass should therefore begin with teaching them the meaning of the signs and symbols and how to participate fruitfully (D 12). To start from something like the Real Presence is to start at the wrong end.

This argues for an early introduction of young children to participation at Mass. Exactly how early we dare not say: that is a decision for those who are dealing daily with the children. The point we are making is that lack of knowledge of the teaching on the Mass is of itself no barrier to participation. The argument often heard is that even five or six year olds are too young for the Mass because they do not understand what is going on. Who does fully understand?

It will be interesting in a few years' time to discover if there has been any significant change in the Catholic's knowledge of the faith. The introduction of the vernacular, the new system of readings, and (we hope) the improvement in the standard of preaching may well bring about a higher level of awareness of what the faith means. This learning process is not a conscious one: it takes place by participating in the Mass consciously and actively.

Much depends upon the priest. It is not only at children's Masses that a great deal of effort should be put into celebration. The vernacular and the simplified ritual have revealed many a foible which, unnoticed in the old liturgy, is glaringly obvious in the new. The celebration of the reformed liturgy is not just a matter of the application of new rules and regulations but of a complete change of attitude. The failure to make this change, or even to recognise that such a change is necessary, is the biggest threat to the new liturgy. As the years go by we may find that the quality of our faith will depend more and more upon the quality of celebration.

The Directory for Masses with Children, without propounding any clear plan, seems to regard two dogmas as necessary for children in their understanding of the Mass - communion and Paschal Mystery. In a sense they are not so much dogmas as themes - a grouping of dogmas.

Communion

Often when a word is used in a restricted technical sense its obvious, wider meaning becomes obscured. 'Communion' is one of these words. For most adult Catholics it conjures up the vision of a long walk up the nave of a church to the altar rail, the reception of the Host and the return to one's place.

Its obvious but often forgotten meaning has a much wider application. The word is made up of two parts -union and 'comm-' which is a prefix meaning 'with'. So communion means union with something or somebody.

That is what sacramental ('holy') communion is all about (cf D 8). By baptism we became one with Christ, and if with Christ, then one body with all the other baptised who are one with him. What baptism begins the Mass and sacramental communion develop and lead towards perfection - complete union which will happen only in heaven. There, Christ and all the baptised will live united in a state of perfect love. Sacramental communion is a pledge of that perfect union yet to come.

First Communion instruction should be based upon that fact (D 12). Traditionally, most First Communion instruction has been based upon the doctrine of the Real Presence; but that is only part of the reality. Real Presence - what for? For union with Christ and the whole Church. When a child makes his First Communion he is not primarily making an act of faith: he is performing an action. The act of faith comes before, often months, even years, before the act of First Communion. When the child receives Christ in communion for the first time he is using an already pre-existing act of faith to help him understand his new-found union with Christ and the Church. Therefore over-emphasis on the Real Presence is bad for the doctrine of the Real Presence – because it risks ignoring what the Real Presence is for.

To put it another way: faith in the Real Presence should not be the only requirement for First Communion. For example, what is the difference between paying a private visit to a church where the sacrament is reserved and going to communion at Mass? If the fact of the presence of Christ is the only truth involved, why go to the trouble of communion? The fact is there is more to communion than the simple presence of Christ. The difference between a mere visit and communion lies in what communion *does*.

For a long time now every child, before making his First Communion, has been required to distinguish between ordinary bread and the Body of Christ. Let us retain that requirement, but let us add to it a requirement for the answer to the question, 'Why is bread changed into Christ's Body?' The answer is the gateway to an understanding of the reality of the Church, of what it means to be a member of a community (that word again!). Communion is not just a visit to a spiritual filling station where we receive energy to combat the problems of the coming week. It is the moment when we unite ourselves with the Body of Christ; and that Body is made up of everybody who has been baptised. From this flows awareness of what the Church is, who Christ is. From the act of communion arises commitment and responsibility to a community, and a new and deeper relationship to every man, woman and child in the Church.

Naturally your ten year old will not grasp all that until he has grown older and matured. Yet the fundamentals are surprisingly similar to the child's own experience of family life. His experience of family life is very real to him and is his guarantee of security. He is already learning that family life calls for effort and cooperation from each member in such a way that their love (or lack of it) can build (or destroy) the harmony of the home.

The Mass builds up the body of the Church. Communion and all the other acts of participation bring about a deeper sharing in the life of Christ and it creates an awareness of the Church's obligation to proclaim God's Word. A proclamation that is by word and example.

The truth that the Mass unites us with Christ and the community is the foundation upon which all else is built. To be united with others in the Mass must mean that we believe essentially what they believe. Not that each member of Christ's Mystical Body believes exactly the same way as every other member. The content of a child's faith must necessarily be different from that of a trained theologian, just as a child's love needs time to become as self-sacrificing as his parents'.

The faith of the individual constitutes what we can call 'motives for action'. In other words, Christ did not teach us about the Kingdom of Heaven so that we could nod our heads sagely and say, 'How very interesting'. No, Christ taught us those truths so that we would act, so that we would use our powers to help in the spreading of the gospel.

Therefore when we teach children 'the faith' we are teaching them to live. A series of dry truths is not enough, wonderful as those truths may be. Truth makes us act differently. The Directory makes this very clear in D 15. Indeed that short paragraph might well be written up in every home and school and printed as the foreword to every catechism.

Living the gospel means living the truths taught by Christ. When we teach children about the Mass we should teach them in such a way that they will live differently than they did before. That difference will be felt most of all at communion. Participation in the Mass should make all of us feel and act differently about Christ and his members (D 55).

Paschal Mystery again

Children have been redeemed. The passion, death and resurrection of Christ have caused them to die and to live a new life in Christ, as much as priest or pope, parent or teacher. Children are Christians and should live as if it meant something to them. The Directory tells us (D 8) that the full Christian life cannot be lived without participation in the liturgy which makes present the Paschal Mystery. The conclusion is inescapable: participation in the liturgy is essential for the Christian life of children also.

If the Paschal Mystery is essential to the Christian life, and if that Mystery is made present in the liturgy, then children should be taught what it means. It is a notion as old as Judaism and is the most fundamental truth of the Christian faith - yet this writer had never heard the phrase until long after his ordination to the priesthood. Which says something for Vatican II being a re-discovery of the faith for many of us.

Paschal Mystery means the Passing Over. The Passing from slavery to freedom, from death to life, from sin to salvation. The first Passover was accomplished when Moses led out of Egypt those who had been signed with the blood of the paschal lamb. The final Passover is accomplished when we are all signed with the blood of the Lamb who is Christ. Passover, or Paschal Mystery, is also closely linked with communion. The first Passover in Egypt united the Hebrews as a nation and started them on their way to the Promised Land. The Passover of Christ unites us all as members of one family and starts us on our way to the heavenly Jerusalem, which is God's kingdom.

Too much theology for young children? Maybe: but no more than the desiccated truths of the Penny Catechism. The Paschal Mystery is what dogmatic definitions are all about, but it has the advantage of being the story of a real life lived long ago and a real life that we should live now because it still goes on in the Mass.

Chapter 5

AT MASS WITH THE GROWN-UPS

A special Sunday Mass for children is an attractive proposition. At least, it is until you begin to plan it and to decide at what time it should be held. Then it is that the difficulties begin to be apparent.

Of all the Masses a child attends, the vast majority are for grown-ups. Sunday Mass with the family is the normal Mass for the average Catholic youngster.

Nor can anyone predict which Mass on a given Sunday will be attended by the majority of children. That factor depends upon such imponderables as the time each family went to bed the night before, how long it took to have breakfast, last-minute crises over clean clothes, what the weather is like, and which church particular families choose to attend. The days of strict attendance at one's own parish church vanished at the advent of our modern mobile society.

Rarely can a priest accurately predict the Mass at which there will be the greatest child attendance; the exceptions in a few notable parishes serve merely to prove the rule. Rarely, too, is there the possibility of sufficient preparation for a full-scale Sunday children's Mass. Preparation, that is, of all the children with the celebrant.

This is not necessarily a bad thing. Sunday Mass is a family affair. Each family, the young and the old together, comes with all its joys and its sorrows, its needs and its thanksgivings to the God who is Father of all. The sense of community should override any sectional interest. At the same time we do not wish to deny the value of the occasional

Sunday Mass which focuses upon a particular group within the community: what we wish to avoid is the regular celebration, Sunday by Sunday, which breaks up the worship of the family as family.

Equally to be avoided is the Mass which ignores the children altogether. D 16 to D 19 offer some suggestions of what to do for them during what is basically an adult Mass. The important basis of these suggestions is that they make use of the liturgy itself. It was not so very long ago that the Sunday Children's Mass was really two liturgies going on at the same time and in the same place: one for the priest and one for children who were led in specially composed prayers by a lay volunteer or a teaching Sister. The Directory is anxious that children be involved in the very action of the Mass itself.

Broadly speaking, there are three ways to encourage children's participation in the Mass:

1. Occasional words addressed to them by the celebrant
2. Special involvement in the actions and gestures of the Mass
3. A Mass completely adapted to their needs.

Option 3 need not detain us long here. While admitting the possibility of such a Mass on occasional Sundays, there are a number of questions to be asked—

Such a Mass should be thoroughly prepared by all the children; how is this to be done? Adaptation on a large scale means adaptation to a particular age group: Which group? Why one rather than another?

What happens to the grown-ups meanwhile? How can they participate?

Given the possibility of such Masses being celebrated in the local schools, is it necessary to have them also on Sundays? How are the children to grow accustomed to the adult celebration?

The family is the best teacher. A child learns much by imitating his parents: they have greater power than anyone else. Mothers and fathers are endowed by their children with near-magical powers and are faultless in their eyes. Therefore learning to pray at Mass, knowing when to stand, sit or kneel, how to pay attention etc., comes more easily to the child who habitually attends Mass alongside his mother and father. And just as important is the sense of community which must arise if the family worships together: it is a sense which as the child grows older will take in the rest of the community. The eucharist creates community, but it is also a question of a lived experience. That experience can start with the family and move out from there.

The problem of 'with whom?' the child celebrates the Sunday Mass leads on naturally to the problem of 'with what?' - the form of the Sunday liturgy. The Directory was written so that the Mass might be adapted to the needs of children. But beware! The Directory does not state that each and every Mass at which children are present should be adapted to their needs. Far from it.

Children remain children for a remarkably short period of time. In no time at all they are grown-up and mature. Education tries to prepare them for maturity. Likewise the Directory for Mass with Children is concerned with introducing children to a fuller participation in the adult form of the Mass (D 21). It would be disastrous to do otherwise because that would have the result of building a barrier between the child and adult worlds.

By means of a careful application of the Directory, children will be better equipped to understand and participate in adult liturgy. They will not be thus equipped if they have not had the experience of regular participation in adult liturgies. A danger to avoid is imprisoning children in a world of children's liturgy. A mother who treats her fifteen year old as if he were a five year old is all set for tragedy.

Nor must we forget the teaching power of the entire community (cf D 11). There is a power, an impressive spirituality in a parish participating in the Sunday Mass; a power which can have a deep effect upon the child. It is an experience of the living Church in action, and this is more effective when the adults are united in a form of the Mass truly expressive of their maturity both as human beings and as Christians.

The Mass is for the community, not any one section of it (cf D 12). There are many occasions when adaptation of the liturgy for a particular group seems desirable, but when all groups meet together at the Sunday liturgy then the general form of the Mass should be the one which suits the majority.

What can be done

Having said all that, it does not follow that the priest is being recommended to do nothing at all for children at Sunday Mass. As in all other things, extreme positions in liturgical matters result in faulty judgements.

Let us say straightaway that a Mass at which a substantial number of those present are children should never be without some adaptation or help for those children. Such a Mass directed exclusively to the needs of adults is as great an offence against the community as a completely adapted children's Mass with an eighty per cent adult congregation.

The needs of the children demand that the adults make some concession to their presence and participation. Ways of doing this on a regular, Sunday by Sunday basis will be examined below. But is there a case to be made for an *occasional* Mass wholly adapted to the needs of children, using the adaptations of Chapter III of the Directory?

Yes, but only on rare occasions. Such a Mass requires careful and prolonged preparation. This applies not merely to the celebrant of the Mass but also to the children, and they cannot be well prepared unless they are members of an already existing group. For example, a children's Mass, making use of all the options, would probably be a failure if celebrated on a routine Sunday for the children who happen to turn up that day and at that time. On the other hand, if the children are celebrating their First Communion and all hail from the same school where they have been carefully prepared, then the conditions would be right for such a Mass.

Young children are experts at looking bright and saying all the right things 'for Father', and at the same time not understanding a jot of what is going on. Specialised liturgies can all too often become self-delusion for the celebrant. Thorough preparation is the only answer.

There also exist some lesser difficulties in the way of a completely adapted Sunday Mass. The first of these concerns the number of children participating in the Mass (D 28). A large number can be self-defeating, because no matter how good children are they find it a great strain to refrain from talking and laughing amongst themselves when in a large group. This is not naughtiness: it is of the nature of children. Nor do we advocate total silence and grim looks, but in a large group this can get out of control so that the priest loses the attention of his congregation.

A further difficulty concerns ages. Ideally the children participating in their adapted Mass should be of the same age group or same educational level. In that way the adaptations can be more easily tailored. At a Sunday Mass this is not easy. But that is not to say it is impossible. The Directory, if intelligently used, can provide a suitably adapted Mass for a wide range of ages.

Ruling out the fully-adapted children's Mass as a regular, Sunday by Sunday occurrence, is not to say that children should be abandoned to their fate. Far from it.

A parish with a large number of young children should have at least one Sunday Mass each week which pays special attention to them. Before considering folk Masses, Latin Masses and the like, the priest should cater for the youngsters of five to eleven (cf D 11 and 19).

Choose the same time each Sunday, prepare carefully and the results will exceed expectations. The news will spread around the parish, and parents and children will come in droves. After a while an experienced nucleus of children will be built up and so more ambitious liturgies can be attempted.

At what age should they begin going to Mass?
No definite rule can be laid down about the age at which children should begin going to Mass. Certainly it is desirable that they should be accustomed to Mass-going before they first go to school. If not, there is a risk that the child will associate going to Mass with going to school, and the result when he leaves school may be calamitous.

The Directory refers to 'Infants who are unable or unwilling' (D 16). The use of the term 'infants' indicates the fact that *very* young children are being referred to; toddlers in fact. To be 'unable' to participate is a good criterion of unreadiness for worship. Only the parents can make a judgement in this matter, but they should remember that there are degrees of participation. The Directory does not demand hundred per cent participation as a condition for attendance at Mass.

The judgement of the parents is applicable also to the

'unwilling' child. There is no sense in forcing a child to Mass. Of course, there are frequent occasions when a child is merely trying to assert himself against his parents; but that is not being considered here. More important is the problem of the child who, through some deep-seated fear or aversion, finds Mass-going a severe trial. In such cases the parents must be patient and wait until their own example has had its influence. Ill-advised is the priest who interferes here.

ADAPTATIONS AT SUNDAY MASS

The possibilities for Sunday Mass are many. Here are the principal ones.

1. *'Unable or unwilling' infants* (D 16)
This is not really an adaptation of the Mass itself. The Directory suggests that children who cannot participate in the Mass be left in the care of a group of 'child-minders' in a room or hall apart from the church. This is not altogether new but it is not yet common.

What is much more common is the 'crying room' - a glassed-in, sound-proofed section of the church for mothers with crying babies. Such a solution has the obvious advantage of leaving the baby under its mother's control, and yet she is able to see what is going on at Mass. But there are disadvantages. First, the mother is unable to participate because no matter how relieved the congregation may be at the sudden silencing of the crying baby, *she* still has to put up with it. In some cases she might just as well go home. Second, very many mothers object to their exclusion from the church. The glass wall is an iron curtain which they resent.

More realistic is the Directory's suggestion of child-minders. Parents are able to attend Mass together without the distraction of a very young, bored child. Naturally there are difficulties, the chief one being that strangers look after the child for the duration of the Mass. But since many parents do not object to relatively unknown baby-sitters in their own homes this objection is not a strong one.

The during-Mass care of children needs to be well organised. The first requirement is a large room close enough to the church for quick and efficient communication between the two places, yet far enough away to suppress any crying or shouting the children might make.

The second requirement is a group of people willing and able to spare time for the baby-minding. On a Sunday this is not so easy. Married people naturally have other things to do, and elderly parishoners often do not have the strength to cope with a struggling infant. The choice seems to fall fairly and squarely upon the teenage girls of the parish.

This Sunday task fits snugly into the parish youth club's community service programme. An intensive course in child care from a nurse or mother would not only give the girls the necessary skills but it would provide them with a practical pre-training for later life. This training (even if lasting only one evening) is essential for the safety of the children and the peace of mind of the parents.

There is more to this, however. Not only is the scheme designed for babies but also for older children who will be much more mobile and in need of entertainment. Here we are verging on the world of the organised play-group which is such a feature of our urban society. If the local play-group has its premises next to the church (as many in fact have) it would surely need little persuasion of the organisers to allow the premises to be opened on Sundays for one hour. Otherwise money must be spent on a few items of play equipment, or toys be allocated from the parish.

Added to the group's fun and games there should be an

element of prayer and religious teaching. That it will be of the very simplest kind goes without saying, but it will need thought and preparation.

The end of each Sunday session is marked by taking the children into the church for the final blessing at the end of the Mass (D 16). This serves as an 'event' for the children, a collecting point for parents and a realisation by the whole community of what is being done behind the scenes to make the Mass more enjoyable.

2. *Words only* (D 17)

If, say, a quarter of the congregation at a particular Sunday Mass does not understand his adult language, the celebrant should take the trouble to speak specially to that quarter at two or three points in the Mass. The first occasion is during the Introduction. After explaining the theme to the grown-ups only, a few words are required to give the children a theme of their own. It will not always be the same theme as the adults; it is best to make it something concrete and easily recognisable.

The conclusion of the homily is another point at which the children can be reminded of the theme. If the celebrant is a good planner he will sometimes be able to delay the climax of his adult homily until he speaks to the children. In that way the children feel part of the main homily, and the adults are left in no doubt about its aim.

To balance the Introduction and homily it follows that the conclusion of the Mass (before the Blessing) is another appropriate moment to speak to the children. Here they need some thought, some idea or resolution to take away with them. It is most effective when it is the same theme as the Introduction and homily: too many ideas lead to confusion.

Should we add to the number of 'interventions' for

children? Probably not. After all we are speaking here of adult Masses: the addition of more children's elements would alter the character of the celebration.

3. *Action* (D 18)

Words alone are not enough for the liturgical participation of children. They also need something to do, movement, physical action. To a lesser extent, this applies to grown-ups too. The problem is far greater for young children, and no amount of talking at them, even in words and terms they can understand, will substitute for judiciously selected participation in the movement of the liturgy.

The Directory offers two examples. The first is the *Offertory Procession*, and there is no doubt that this is one of the most useful parts children can play in the Mass. What is especially important is that the Offertory is not a peripheral element in the Mass - it is of its very heart. At the same time it is physically central, in that the entire action of celebrant and congregation ceases while the Procession is in progress. In other words, the children do not have the impression of being given something to do to 'keep them happy': they are playing a real and important part in the liturgical action. Furthermore they are concerned with the bread and wine - the most essential elements in the Mass.

The Directory's second example is *singing*. Getting a children's choir together is not the easiest thing in the world and some might have doubts about its advisability. Too often a children's choir has been a source of irritation to adults because of the behaviour of the children in between their sung contributions. But that need not be so, and indeed such behaviour is often the fault of adult directors who are so intent upon the music that every other part of the liturgy is completely forgotten. If the choir is placed at the front of the church, or at any rate where it can feel itself to be part of the community, then many of these difficulties disappear (cf G[1] 274).[1]

The music facilities of primary schools have improved enormously in recent years. In particular, instrumental music plays a greater part in the lives of quite young children. Here, then, is yet another source of participation in the Mass: a small but ambitious group of instrumentalists can add an air of solemnity and originality to the occasional Sunday celebration. Recorders, glockenspiel, chime-bars and, of course, guitars are all fairly commonly found in the competent hands of children. Even the more difficult stringed instruments, such as the violin, form part of many a school's musical education.

Apart from choral work some children might be trained as soloists to sing the responsorial psalm, or any other such psalmodic chant. Admittedly this is far more ambitious and only a few children are capable of this, particularly as we are here concerned with children of eleven years and under. But it has been done with great success.

Closely connected with the singing of chants are the *readings*. The clear voice of a child is often better than the gruff growl of an adult. Nervousness appears to be less of a problem with the youngster than with others of more mature years. Children are accustomed to reading out loud at school and still have this training fresh in their minds.

However there is one objection to this practice. The readings at Mass are not to be read but proclaimed, and there is a big difference between the two. Proclamation implies contributing something of one's own faith and experience. Can a young child have such faith and experience? Or is it rather a parrot-fashion repetition? If the latter, then the

1. GI: General Instruction on the Roman Missal, Rome, 1969. English translation by Clifford Howell S.J., C.T.S., London.

child should not read. A recording of Laurence Olivier would serve the same purpose - and better.

The Word is a living thing in which God still speaks to his people. It requires that he who reads be one imbued with the faith contained in that reading. He should be an instrument of the living Word and not just a repeater of the printed word. Which is not to say that it is impossible for children to read at Masses for adults. While many of the Sunday readings are undoubtedly difficult there are others which, with help from priest, parent or teacher, are easily comprehensible to the young reader.

The *Prayers of the Faithful* (Bidding Prayers) especially lend themselves to reading by children at an adult Mass. Their advantage is that their texts may be simplified to suit the children. That does not in any way imply a watering-down of the content. Some of the turgid prayers heard in many places would benefit from such simplification. Occasionally the prayers might be written by the children themselves. However this implies a comprehension of the gospel theme which is normally beyond the powers of youngsters who have heard the reading only once; the Prayers of the Faithful are intended to be a prayerful response to God's Word. Yet the possibility is there.

An attractive alternative is the composition of the prayers by an entire family. Naturally this implies a limited amount of Bible study and discussion within the family: that is a good thing in itself, particularly if the local priest takes trouble to help and advise each family. Some form of rota would encourage many families to deepen their interest in and knowledge of the liturgy.

Traditionally, boys have always had a part to play in the Mass through serving; *serving at Mass* is a most important as well as practical form of participation. Much has been said of the supposed down-grading of the server in the light of the recent liturgical reforms. Such criticism is unfounded. The General Instruction of the new Roman Missal gives the server a liturgical/theological standing not officially accorded him before. What has really happened is that local parishes have failed to understand the reforms and have themselves all but eliminated the function of the server. Not only children, but the liturgy itself demands movement and ceremonial. The liturgical reforms offer abundant opportunities for these important elements, but sadly many priests have failed to realise the opportunities presented to them.

And what of girls? For too long the public image of the Church was male-oriented: women were for convents and pews. Now attitudes are changing. Women and girls are allowed to read at Mass. The next male fortress would appear to be in the matter of serving; after all, if a woman is allowed to be an extraordinary minister of holy communion, why not a Mass server too? Whatever the merits of this argument, priests should ensure that girls receive fair treatment within the limits of what is allowable. Although sometimes the greatest examples of male chauvinism seem to come from women themselves!

Participation in the Mass need not be confined to action within the Mass; there are ways of *participation by preparing for the Mass*. Many a dull church would be enlivened by the addition of a poster, or series of posters, designed and executed by the children from the local school. These are particularly successful at the more important liturgical seasons such as Christmas, Easter and Pentecost. Making the posters, or wall-hangings, could constitute the practical part of the teaching on the liturgical seasons of the year at the local school, as well as being a valuable lesson for the grown-ups. This is but one of many ways in which children can take part 'in anticipation'. The decoration of a church is as important to the liturgy as any other form of participation.

A warning. Much as we may be interested in the involvement of children in the Sunday or Holy day Mass, let us not forget that we are discussing Masses which are basically for adults. A full-blown children's Mass is another matter entirely. Therefore we must never allow the children to take over all the possible elements of participation. The adults have as much right to participation as anybody else and should be allowed to exercise that right. In our eagerness to help our children let us not get things out of proportion.

4. *Special Liturgy of the Word* (D 17)

The Directory has a suggestion for children at adult Masses which has been successfully tried in many places - that there sometimes be a Liturgy of the Word for children totally distinct from the adult's. Basically this means that the children have readings, homily and Prayers of the Faithful designed for their own needs, in a place completely separated from the grown-ups.

The advantages of this idea are obvious. Both readings and homily can be tailored and simplified directly to the needs of the children. It demands the need for more personnel and space but that should not be beyond the resources of a medium-sized parish.

This is what happens. After the Opening Prayer of the adult Mass the children are led from the church to a nearby hall or room. There they are in the charge of another priest, or catechist, who presides at the simplified readings, delivers the homily and directs the Prayers of the Faithful. All these are arranged beforehand to be at the level of the majority of children taking part. That is the basic plan: carrying it out demands much thought and organisation.

First, let us examine the liturgical side of it. A mad rush of children at the conclusion of the Opening Prayer is undignified; their departure should be part of the liturgy.

This can be done by the catechists shepherding the children, two by two. Or (and this is preferable) by some movement from the sanctuary of the church. For example: three servers come forward, two with lighted candles, and the third with the children's lectionary which he has taken from the altar where it has been lying since the Entry Procession. The celebrant blesses the server holding the lectionary, the party of three leave the sanctuary, processes down the centre of the church, and all the other children follow. In this way an atmosphere of dignity and order is produced which is of benefit not only to the remaining adults, but also to the children when they enter the nearby hall.

Once in the hall the liturgical atmosphere must at all costs be maintained. It is not a playtime. This is prepared for by grouping the chairs around some focal point (not an altar, since this is not the Liturgy of the Eucharist); it will probably be a lectern suitably decorated, and alongside which the servers place their candles. Close to the lectern, a chair for the leader.

The readings, though simplified, should be carried out with solemnity, with a sense of liturgy. The simplification, the possibilities of the homily (dialogue with the children, use of drama, of illustrations etc.) are all described in Chapter 8.

Full use can be made of the adaptations for Masses where only a few adults are present.

The children's Bidding Prayers concluded, all process back into the church, led by the servers. It is a good idea for the first three or four children to pick up the Offerings so that the returning procession becomes the Offertory Procession.

Finally the children return to their places in the church.

Timing is important. The adults must not be kept waiting, otherwise their own celebration loses its rhythm. The pace should be set by the adult Liturgy of the Word, and someone posted at a connecting door to keep a co-ordinating eye on both liturgies is obviously essential. Previous planning carried out by the leaders of both liturgies is also very important.

The organisation of those adults who are to be with the children during the Liturgy of the Word is probably the first step. One person is not enough: a proportion of one adult to every ten children does not seem excessive. It is a good plan to ensure that each adult has some idea of the theme to be followed and of any special actions the children might be required to make. The sort of adults for this task are, naturally, catechists, teachers or a few parents. The local youth club is often a source of enthusiastic and reliable help.

The children require as much careful selection as the adult helpers. It is difficult to make the division, but probably the very young (toddlers) are best left out of this form of the liturgy. They will understand as little of the children's Liturgy of the Word as of the adult's and will be a distraction to other children. By and large, this form of the liturgy is more useful for the child of six to eleven years of age. It may be possible to subdivide the children into age groups when the hall or room has been reached, but this method presents difficulties of its own.

Such a liturgy, as we have described it, will be of particular benefit in areas where many children do not attend Catholic schools. Detailed planning for weeks ahead can provide a 'syllabus' of graduated instruction for these children.

It is worth being aware that some parents may object to all of this. They may feel that their children should stay with them throughout the entire course of the Mass. Persuasion can be tried, but, if unsuccessful, such parents should not be made to feel liturgical outcasts. It is their right to make such a decision.

Further points. If a priest is the leader of the children's group then it is suitable that he also concelebrate the Mass. At the conclusion of the Mass, the celebrant briefly reminds the children of what they celebrated in their Liturgy of the Word. Some prefer that the children be allotted special places in the church, away from the grown-ups: this has advantages from the organisational point of view but it is not so satisfactory as far as the family unit is concerned. It is also possible that the children be led from the church immediately after the Greeting and Introduction and before the Penitential Rite. Attractive as this sounds, allowing the possibility of a specially adapted Penitential Rite and Collect, it does not give the children enough time to become part of the main community. The Penitential Rite is the act of reconciliation of the entire community and is not as susceptible of division as is the Liturgy of the Word.

A note on full-scale adaptation of Sunday Mass
The decision to make use of the more extensive adaptations contained in Chapter III of the Directory is not the local clergy's. It is reserved to the bishop (D 19). At first sight this is alarming, but we should call to mind the manner in which most bishops work today.

Each diocese has a liturgical commission which acts in the name of the bishop. Its function is to be informed about the theology and history of the liturgy, about the latest documentation, from Rome or from the National Commission, about modern trends in liturgical thought and practice, and about the liturgical state of the diocese which it serves. In this way it advises the bishop on all liturgical matters and is his normal means of communication of liturgical material to the diocese.

A parochial priest who is confronted with a problem about the extent of adaptation for children necessary on Sundays should contact the liturgical commission of his diocese. The views of the commission are based upon a wider knowledge of the diocese, of the Directory, and of children - most commissions include members of the diocese's catechetical team. In this way the priest obtains not only the permission he requires but also a good deal of practical guidance in putting the permission into operation.

That, of course, is the ideal. How many diocesan commissions actually work that way? Perhaps more than many people realise. But a commission cannot function properly unless it is used by those whom it is meant to serve. Many a commission has floundered because the parochial clergy has neglected it.

Responsibility too falls upon the shoulders of the commission members. It is their duty to be well-informed on a wide spectrum of liturgical matters, and this requires both serious study and a willingness to go into the diocese to find out what is going on. A passing interest in rubrics (as an offshoot of canon law) is not enough.

Chapter 6

SCHOOL AND GROUP

Speak of children's Masses and there is one phrase that is bound to occur! Classroom Masses. At least, that is so in the British Isles. While there has long existed a need for adapted Masses for children on Sundays, the most experimentation and the loudest appeals for permission to adapt the Mass have come from the classrooms.

The word 'classroom' appears nowhere in the Directory, but he is a dull man indeed who would deny that the concept of the classroom Mass fits perfectly Chapter III of the Directory. It is the longest chapter in the Directory (D 20 to 54), contains the most basic adaptations, and is built upon the simple premise of children's Masses celebrated with only a few adults present. Where is that premise more clearly verified than in the school classroom?

Yet we should not be exclusive in the application of this part of the Directory. Already we have seen the possibilities of the full adaptation of an occasional Sunday parochial Mass. Other possibilities exist: regular Masses for boarding schools, for scouts, for girl guides, for First Communion, even for Confirmation. The list is not exhaustive, but the classroom remains the one place in which Chapter III of the Directory can most easily be applied. Indeed, a large amount of the material consulted by the commission which wrote the Directory came from the classrooms of the world.

A word of caution: a classroom Mass need not always be celebrated in a classroom. Its preparation takes place there but it could be celebrated in any place - church, school assembly hall, school library, or anywhere judged to be worthy and convenient. Later we will discuss the choice of site in more detail; what is important now is that the developing preparation of the Mass be seen to be ideally located in one small group of children with their teacher in their classroom (cf D 25).

Preparation is essential for success. We must resist the temptation to cut corners, attempting to introduce adaptations which the children do not expect. Playing with adaptations is the new strain of the disease long known to the Church as rubricism. The celebration of Mass by a group of children should be the logical outcome of what they have already learned and celebrated in many different ways in the classroom.

Guide-lines for the preparation of a children's Mass are not easily laid down. Some of them are more conveniently discussed when dealing with the actual celebration of the Mass. Therefore we will follow the broad pattern of the Directory by first discussing the people, places and things of the celebration, (D 20 to 37) only later passing on to the form of the celebration (D 38 to D 54).

At the risk of repetition, we feel we should once again remind ourselves what it is we are preparing children for: the individual celebration of the Mass suited to the age and education of the children, yes. But that is not all: our vision must stretch far beyond the single celebration to future celebrations, years hence, when the children are grown up and have children of their own. Our work is to build a worshipping Church, the Body of Christ united sacramentally at the altar. Many a successful celebration will fill us with joy, and rightly so. Never forget, however, that real success is in the hearts and minds of the children and that success cannot be measured in terms of joyful singing, enthusiastic responses, well-composed prayers, but only in terms of closeness to Christ (cf D 20 and D 22).

I. THE CHILDREN

Participation in the liturgy is only as good as the preparation
put into it beforehand. Preparation is a form of participation:
it is the anticipation of celebration.

Good preparation takes time, thought and energy. Nothing
is easier for the busy teacher or priest than to say to a group
of children, 'Tomorrow we are going to have a special
Mass' - and then prepare texts and gestures privately, away
from the distracting influence of the children. Preparation
must be the team action of teacher, priest and children. If
any one of these three is missing then the celebration will
suffer accordingly.

Paradoxically children's liturgical participation is both
difficult and easy. Difficult if the children come to the Mass
with little understanding of the theme, the special gestures,
the readings, and so forth. Easy if they have helped in
choosing the readings, developing the theme, planning processions . . .

Preparation cannot begin too soon (D 29). That is not to
say that the readings or Prayers of the Faithful are to be
chosen or composed weeks before the actual event. Preparation can begin quite unbeknown to teacher, priest and
children. After days or weeks discussing, for example, the
starving people of India it may gradually become clear to
the teacher that the celebration of a special Mass would be
an appropriate climax to the project. The plight of the
Indians, the resources of the richer nations, the words of
scripture about justice, the resulting obligations on each
individual, what practical things the children can do - all
these elements are a form of preparation for the celebration
of a Mass. The final stage of the preparation consists in
translating into liturgical terms the various aspects of the
problem.

Prayers of the Faithful thanking God for our plenty and asking the grace to share with the starving, readings from scripture of what Jesus said about feeding the hungry, an Offertory Procession of gifts destined for the starving of India - these are random examples of planning and preparation which might take a week or more, but only as the conclusion of a much more extensive period of unconscious preparation.

What we are saying here links up directly with our remarks in Chapter 3 about the teacher and celebration. If you can teach it, you can celebrate it. Any class or project can be made into liturgical celebration. The reason is obvious. When we teach children we are teaching them about themselves and the wonderful world God has given them. That is true whether or not God is mentioned or thought of. Teaching is the discovery of material for celebration.

To spend time at the end of a teaching project in the discovery of readings, prayers and gestures which will identify the secular with the religious and vice versa is really what Catholic education is all about. It is this writer's opinion that the failure to make the identification in worship is one of the major reasons for the present lack of confidence in our Catholic school system. Secular subjects can be taught just as well in non-denominational schools, and experience proves that religious instruction can be given to Catholic children in these schools. What can only be done in a denominational school is to lead the secular subject into a living act of worship, showing how all comes to us from God, that all things were created in Christ.

An example taken from a real-life classroom situation will illustrate one way of preparing for celebration. This occurred in a central London primary school with children of average ability.

The project, designed to last through several weeks, was

'Animals'. The entire syllabus was used for the project at various times. The size, weight and speed of various animals were discussed, measured and compared (Mathematics). The life and form of most animals depends upon their habitat, so where do they come from? (Geography). Various animals can be put to use for man - haulage, food, clothing, other raw materials. Animals have a place in history - Alexander's horse, Hannibal's elephants. They play a great part in literature (English).

From all this material it was not difficult for the teacher to show God's goodness in providing nature with so many wonders, and how the children ought to thank and praise God. Not difficult, too, to evoke prayers for the conservation of nature, for a proper care of God's creation. So the children planned a Mass. They chose the readings and wrote the prayers. The classroom was already full of pictures, models and facts and figures about animals. The Mass was a great success.

The Prayers of the Faithful are a good illustration of what the children produced. When discovering animals in literature, the teacher had used the opportunity to explain certain common sayings used in the English language. This is how the children prayed:

'Dear Lord, please help me to have the courage to be as brave as a lion and as strong as an ox, because I will be up against great dangers in my life; so I ask you Lord to give me these things.

'Dear Lord, help me to be as happy as a lark when lots of things have gone wrong, and help me to cheer up other people.

'Father give us happiness. May we all be as bright as a lark.

'Dear Lord, I ask you to make me as wise as an owl so that

I can understand and learn a lot at school and maybe go to college.

'Dear Lord, let us be as busy as bees, never lazy but helping others with their work and doing our own work.

'Dear Lord, I ask you to make me as gentle as a lamb and never to fight any of my friends. You know how a lamb is so gentle that it would never hurt anyone. Well make me like that.'

There is a simplicity and straightforwardness about these prayers which is closer to the heart of real prayer than many grown-up efforts. Most of all the children have used their 'secular' classwork in the service of the liturgy.

The children who produced these prayers (and prepared the other parts of the Mass) learned a valuable lesson. They saw how God cares for man through nature, through so many things that man takes for granted. But that care cannot be separated from God's most astounding act of care - the incarnation, death and resurrection of his Son. In the Mass, these children brought together these two apparently unrelated signs of God's goodness and thanked God for his continuing love of man. Discovering the wonders of the animal world, these children found something to celebrate - and they did.

Of course, it is far easier to celebrate religious subjects. A Mass in honour of our Lady after a class has spent some time finding out about her seems the most logical thing in the world. Many schools have a system whereby each week one class prepares the daily assembly, following a specific theme. That amounts to a series of five non-eucharistic liturgies. What would be easier than to plan a class Mass based on these assemblies?

Participation involves everybody. That is why everybody responds to the priest's greeting, why they stand, sit, or kneel at certain times. It is just as important that *all* the children have a part in the preparation. It is a sure method of creating interest in the liturgy, apart from any educational benefits. A busy teacher might be tempted to leave the work to a chosen few, but that way out should be avoided at all costs. Liturgy is the worship not of a faceless crowd but of individuals who comprise a community. It may not always be possible for each child to do something 'special' during the Mass, but the astute teacher will be able to think up ways and means of involving everybody in the preparation.

Easier said than done, of course. Or is it? Later on we will examine many things which require preparation. D 22 gives a preview of these: we add a few more suggestions of our own.

a. *Flowers*
Not essential – certainly not on the altar. But frequently a few fresh flowers create a sense of festivity, of celebration. They are the type of thing that children delight in bringing to school.

b. *The room*
The pinning-up of their own paintings, the preparation of a theme scrap-book, the arrangement of the furniture – all examples of activities in which many children can become involved (D 29).

c. *Vestments*
Making a vestment and seeing it worn by the priest often has a great impact upon the children. This is where the sewing class and the Mass relate together. A chasuble is a simple shape to cut out. The material need not be expensive: a simple white cotton would do. A cross, or some other design, cut out of felt and sewn to the chasuble looks very fine.

The more ambitious might like to cut out various figures representing the Mass theme and sew them to the chasuble. Wearing this during the Mass, the priest shows quite clearly the connection between the 'work of our redemption' and the work of the children. True, many a priest might find it hard to lay aside his 'churchy' chasuble; and some might regard the children's creation as undignified. But dignity is relative. The joy and pride of the children should be enough to convince the wavering priest.

We will have more to say about vestments when discussing the priest's own preparation.

d. *Bread*

The bread for Mass (in the Latin church anyway) must still be unleavened. But that does not mean that it should be the plastic-looking white discs to which we have become so accustomed. Unleavened bread can be much thicker and 'chewier'. This is no stunt.

Jesus took bread, the staple, basic food, and changed it into the Bread of Life. It was a question of an easily recognisable sign (and reality) being changed into another. Today it is difficult to see our familiar white hosts as bread. It would be a great educational exercise for a class to bake some unleavened bread and later witness its use at Mass. The simple lesson is that God takes the ordinary things of life and uses them for our salvation. That is a basic truth clearly shown in the Offertory.

e. *Music* (D 30)

A child without a song is a child without joy. We grown-ups may not always like what and the way they sing but this is certainly a case where the spirit counts; for song is a sign of joy and celebration. Many of our schools place great importance upon a musical training as part of the child's general education, and so it is no difficulty to provide songs and even instrumental music at Mass.

Music, whether sung or played, gives a new dimension to a celebration, and this applies to secular events as well as religious. All sorts of events gain in importance and dignity when a little music is added; the band at a military parade, the interval music at a cinema and the songs at Mass are all related and fulfil the same function. But in addition, the music at Mass provides a new element of participation: all the children can prepare for this and take part.

The only danger is that the music might predominate (as we remarked in the case of children's music at an adult Mass). Music is an integral part of celebration, but it must not be allowed to dominate. During the time of preparation care should be taken to ensure that each Mass contains other elements of participation, apart from music. This is a thing to watch in classes whose teacher is also the school's music expert! At the same time musical participation at Mass can be a challenge for the children. Force of circumstances dictates that much of their musical life at school is for the young musicians' own entertainment: to produce music, sung or instrumental, for the celebration of Mass is a much more outward-going exercise. Singers, recorder players, violinists, pianists, guitarists, percussionists can all find a new role to play at Mass (cf D 32).

The difficulty in providing suitable music for some parts of the Mass has been remarked by many. It is said that the official texts are not susceptible to musical settings. Yet this overlooks an Instruction which the Directory reminds us of once again (D 31). As long ago as 1967 it was officially stated that other written texts can be used so as to accommodate the music more easily (Instruction on Music in the Liturgy, n 55). Gloria, Credo, Sanctus and Agnus Dei need not provide insurmountable difficulties for attractive musical settings.

This is all very well for the teacher with at least a modicum of musical ability, and for a class old enough to do it, but sometimes these requirements are just not present. Then maybe recorded music is the answer (cf D 32). Tapes for accompaniment have been available for three to four years, and there is no lack of music to provide a prayerful background at carefully selected points in the Mass. The same rules against excessive use apply as in the case of live music, but a careful choice of music can also be most helpful at moments of silent prayer, for processions, or for dramatisation of readings.

f. *Local customs* (D 22)
This innocent-looking phrase is our justification in law for many comments and suggestions found in these pages (e.g. Bread, and Vestments, above). The Directory is intended to direct, not dictate. The days are past when Roman documents stipulated each and every item in the liturgy. This Directory is at pains to preserve the essential structure of the Mass (cf D 38) and certain textual features (cf D 39), but it allows a wide liturgical interpretation within and between these compulsory elements.

Children differ the world over. Culture, education, age, intelligence - these are so varied that no document can lay down detailed rules for all cases. However it is not bureaucratic impossibility but liturgical necessity which demands the application of the principle of local custom.

We repeat again, liturgy is the worship of a particular community, at a particular place and time. While preserving the essentials, the liturgy is the expression of the worship of real people, not the application of rubrics. This Directory respects that principle: let us respect the Directory.

Teachers and priests should therefore be open to suggestions from all quarters. Good sense will often judge their worth. In difficult cases the diocesan liturgical commission should be consulted and the matter debated with liturgists and educationalists.

A note about cultural differences
Christ became man to save all men. Man's response has to be that of the whole man - body and soul. The liturgy perfectly expresses this fact in sacramental form: it is made up of the visible and invisible, the physical and spiritual. To be true to the incarnation we must be true to both aspects of the sacramental liturgy (D 33).

Children have more of the physical: their intellectual powers are a long way from full development. Planning of the children's Mass must include special consideration of this fact: the entire Directory is the application of this truth. However, D 33 briefly mentions the application of the same principle to adults in rather special cases, and we should say something about it here.

Cultures differ widely, yet the Latin liturgy is the liturgy of the West. Experiments are well under way to adapt the liturgy to different cultural forms so that it will be a more complete response of particular groups. Africa is feeling its way forward and in India experimentation is well advanced. It follows from this that any children's liturgy in those areas should also be adapated to local cultural patterns. Indeed the Directory suggests that cultural adaptation might be confined to children's liturgy alone. Because of their narrow experience it would be easier for children in these cases to learn to celebrate the Mass by making use of familiar cultural practices. On the other hand, adults in the same area might be required to live in a world of dual cultures; cultural adaptation of the adult Mass would serve merely to emphasise separateness, to create a form of religious ghetto. Hence the strange second paragraph in D 33.

2. THE PRIEST (D 23)

The priest has the power of life and death over a children's Mass. By his own preparation and personality he can lift a mediocre Mass and make it a living liturgy. And, conversely, a well-prepared Mass, looked forward to with eager anticipation by the children, can be ruined by the incomprehension and thoughtlessness of the celebrant. The importance of the priest cannot be overstressed.

What sort of priest has the makings of a good celebrant of children's Masses? One who sees his liturgical role in terms of service - who regards himself as being at the disposal of the congregation for whom he celebrates. The priest is he who feeds the People of God with the Word and the eucharist. His duty is to satisfy the spiritual needs of the community. If the laity did not exist there would be no priesthood.

The priest who is unsuitable for children's Masses is the one who regards the laity as being at the service of the priesthood. For such a priest the most important thing in life is to maintain the dignity of his office. Therefore nothing must occur at children's Mass which in any way appears to detract from his own image of himself. The reader should not regard this as an exaggeration: too many teachers tell hair-raising stories of classroom Mass disasters for us to deny the truth of this.

The second criterion for the suitable priest is a direct consequence of the first. The priest who celebrates a Sunday adult Mass with intelligence, care and understanding of the needs of his congregation is likely to be a good celebrant of Mass for young children.

Yet there is a big difference between children and adults.

Children are not just smaller versions of the grown-up. No matter how good some priests are with adults they feel unable to cope with children. The happy side of this situation is that such priests are usually the first to recognise the problem and will say so.

The priest should be sympathetic towards children, understanding of their limited world of experience, sensitive to their quickly changing moods. His attitude will be fatherly yet not overly protective, not playing the role of 'everybody's daddy'. A common mistake of priests is to treat children with too much affection and to try to be like one of them, often at the expense of the teacher.

On the other hand it is equally a mistake to project the image of a rough, inflexible disciplinarian. This is probably more difficult for the priest who is after all an amateur in education and without children of his own. The noise, movement and interruptions of a modern classroom can be disturbing to the uninitiated. The automatic reaction is to bark and shout and impose the sort of discipline more in keeping with a barracks than a school.

The way to learn is by watching a good teacher at work. Affection and understanding, control and correction are all nicely blended so that while a class of youngsters may be producing a continuing hum of noise and movement the teacher is still in charge. It is an art, but one which can be learned.

Knowing the children
Like the Good Shepherd, the priest should know his own, and his own know him. There is no substitute for being on familiar terms with the children and being instantly recognisable by the children as one who is interested in them. Knowing the names of all the children in a school may not be possible, but faces and characters quickly become

familiar by regular contact. The benefit in the celebration of the children's Mass will be enormous. The celebrant, knowing what sort of children he is dealing with, will be able to strike exactly the right note, say the right word. The relationship established over a lengthy period before the Mass will be deepened by the celebration.

Does it need to be stressed what a great pastoral advantage knowing children can be? Many a priest has gained entry to a home and been able to help solve problems because he first knew the children at the local school. Parents, previously unknown to the priest, have come to him with their difficulties 'because my son told me all about you'. Above all, familiarity with a priest means familiarity with the institutional Church. When they are adults, these children will possess attitudes to the Church and its ministers based upon the knowledge of flesh and blood priests whom they encountered in their formative years.

The priest at school

There is a problem about the role of the priest in the Catholic primary school. The question is: when not celebrating Mass, what should he do there? There was a time when the enthusiastic priest would spend some time formally teaching the children. It was often a blessing for the busy teacher who could use the time thus made available for other tasks. But there was always a doubt about this practice because young children were sometimes confused by the sudden and infrequent appearance of a 'teacher' who interrupted the normal course of the day. Also the ability of the amateur to sustain this type of teaching was extremely dubious.

The introduction of modern educational methods has rendered this form of priest-teaching almost obsolescent. Team teaching and the integrated day do not take kindly to this sort of interruption. 'Put your books away children, and listen to what Father has to say' may be a polite way of saying 'The morning has just been ruined.' That the priest must visit classrooms is certain: how else is he to know all the children and to learn from teachers?

The answer is that the priest should first of all be at the service of the teachers. It is they who know the right moment to speak to the children, who know the timetable, who know when his presence is required, when he can have the greatest impact. Teacher and priest constitute a team for the religious education of the children. Only by working together will they achieve the best results.

Most of the priest's work will be in the staffroom. Recent years have witnessed an apparent conflict between method and content in religious education. Some critics have attacked modern catechetics because they appear to have sacrificed dogmatic content at the altar of teaching method. The result has been a loss of confidence among teachers, and they have not been encouraged by statements made by individuals in authority in our Church who possess neither training nor experience in education. But the local priest is on the spot and he can help.

His duty is one of encouragement, of positive leadership. Through constant contact with a school staff it will not take him long to judge their worth and that of their teaching. He will be able to support the unsure, restrain the unwise. Most important of all, he should be able to lead the teachers to a new knowledge and understanding of the teaching of the Church. At the present time the level of religious lecturing in many colleges of education is not much better than that of the average sixth form; the teachings of Vatican II are still a closed book to the majority. Here lies a rich opportunity for the priest who takes Catholic education seriously: here he will have the most profound influence upon the life of the school.

What teachers demand of a priest is openness, the willingness to listen to another point of view. Simply that a school is situated within a parish boundary, bears the name of Catholic, and includes a priest or two on its board of managers is no justification for clerical domination. Priest and teacher are working for the same ends - the proclamation of the Word of God. This in itself should be enough to break down all barriers and create the right conditions for an open and frank exchange of views. Where this openness exists there is the happy school.

Books, too, are a help to the would-be celebrant of children's Masses. While the priest may learn much from the staff of the school there is much to be gained from reading a book or two describing modern educational and catechetical thinking. Works such as Goldman's *Readiness for Religion*[1] explain in simple terms the application of scientific knowledge about children to the teaching of religion. The findings of such writers bear immediately upon the celebration of Mass for children, and the priest will understand better what is not possible in his use of words, ideas and gestures.

Priest plus children

When a Mass is in its final planning stage the priest should visit the children more frequently. He will be able to advise, clear up difficulties, make suggestions for the celebration. Most important of all, he will be fully aware of the theme and the manner in which it is to be celebrated. The concluding celebration will therefore be a true celebration of all those present, priest as well as children; and it will run smoothly and prayerfully if the priest is already aware of each element in the celebration.

1. Ronald Goldman, *Readiness for Religion*, Routledge and Kegan Paul, London, 1965.

Sometimes the priest must suggest the omission of something which he knows to be unsuitable, but before doing so he must be absolutely sure of his liturgical, theological and educational grounds. Mere dislike is not sufficient. And any objection ought always to be made in the preparation stage before the celebration. Much harm can come from the sweeping aside of prepared items while the Mass is actually in progress. If the objection is carefully explained during one of the priest's preparatory visits the other adults will nearly always appreciate having it pointed out to them.

What the priest uses

The things used by the priest at Mass require careful thought. If the Mass is to take place in a church then much depends upon the size, architecture and general style of that church. If it is to be celebrated in a smaller place, such as a classroom, then the priest has a certain amount of freedom. We will assume that this is in fact the situation.

The first thing to remember is that the size and proportion of congregation and room is considerably smaller than in a church. Therefore the chalice and vestments of a Sunday Mass may be unsuitable. Many chasubles, for instance, were designed for viewing from a distance of up to 100 feet; put the same design in a small room and it creates a feeling of claustrophobia. By its grandeur it overwhelms what is a simple situation.

A simple yet bold design is preferable. It is useful to buy such a vestment because it can be used not only for children's Masses but also for house Masses and similar situations. Some prefer to omit the chasuble, as is permitted by the Instruction on Masses for Small Groups and simply wear an alb and stole. This is a valid alternative but we should remember that we want our children to become accustomed to features of adult Masses, and that they like to see any form of 'dressing up'. For them, the colour and flow of the vestment create a sense of occasion.

For the classroom Mass an ordinary table may be used as the altar (GI 260). Only one cloth is necessary (GI 268) and the altar stone (or antemension) is not required (GI 265). The priest should do his best not to allow the altar to become an ecclesiastical sideboard upon which are placed all sorts of precious little knick-knacks from the church. 'Dignity in simplicity' is the rule. The chalice and paten, solitary in the middle of the cloth's white expanse, will attract attention to the essentials of the Mass more than a cluttered table of bits and pieces.

A paten or bowl-type ciborium for the altar breads will enable all the children to see its contents; functional cruets and a simple chalice add to the dignity of the celebration. A cross is not required on the altar if there is one already hanging in the room (GI 270).

Preparation in the presbytery

Preparation is a thing that starts in the mind. Things are easy enough to prepare: thoughts are more elusive. This holds true not just of children's Masses but of all liturgies with any age-group. The first thought, at least unconsciously, should be, 'This is a celebration'; that is to say, a joyous occasion because it is a thanking of God, through the sacrifice of his Son, for all that he has done for us. It is a celebration of the fact that we all share one life in Christ and have one Father, who is in heaven.

The life of the busy priest sometimes clouds over these ideas. The Mass can all too often be just another part of the daily routine. Therefore there is a need to remind ourselves what it is all about, and although this must be so for all celebrations of the Mass it is especially true of children's Masses. Adults can adjust to different priests and their moods: not so children. That is why the Directory is so insistent upon this point.

It is helpful to think of all the preparation the children have put into the Mass: the excitement they are feeling beforehand. Think too of what they are expecting of the priest and of his vastly magnified standing in their eyes. In other words the priest has to put himself in the mood.

The next bit of mental preparation takes in the fact that this Mass will be with a small group, therefore the atmosphere will be more personal than a Sunday Mass in the parish church. Christian names can be used, individuals spoken to, everybody will be much closer together.

Indeed the atmosphere of a children's Mass is so different that the celebrant must adopt a totally different technique from that on the normal Sunday. The expansive gestures of the big church do not fit into a small room; each one must count and mean something to the young congregation (cf D 33). The spreading of hands and arms at the invitation, 'Let us pray', ought to look like an invitation to prayer, not the exercises of someone trying to keep his weight down. The raising of the hands during the Eucharistic Prayer symbolises the raising of our hearts to God – or is it rather the gesture of a newly-captured prisoner-of-war (cf D 33 and D 34)?

The courageous priest will ask a colleague to attend one of his adult Masses and produce a reasoned criticism of the way he celebrates. This is not playing with peripheral details. The liturgy is made up of signs and symbols which are meaningless unless performed properly. As we remarked earlier, celebrating children's Masses often leads the priest to a revision of his entire attitude to liturgy and its celebration.

Words count as much as gestures. Because of their limited vocabulary children require words which are simple and to the point (cf D 50). It is a hard lesson when, after much effort on our part, a sympathetic teacher tells us that the children have not understood a thing. But persistence pays. Reading a child's story book to oneself is a good way of learning how to express oneself simply.

Above all each introduction and prayer should be prepared. Some find it easier to do this in writing; seeing the phrase helps eliminate complicated and unnecessary words. But during the celebration, scripts should be put aside if possible.

Brevity is the key. A child's level of concentration is remarkably short, particularly when all he can do is listen. TV programmes for the younger child contain very useful indications of how soon the talking must stop. Added to brevity is directness – a directness which demands a response. In a church the celebrant's words tend to be addressed to some mythical being in the back row, and it would certainly be infra dig for someone spontaneously to respond. With children it is different. The celebrant speaks to a small group, to individuals in that group, and he must expect (and even encourage) sudden and surprising interventions. This of course, is genuine participation and may be a sign that the priest has found the right level. More will be said of this when we discuss the separate parts of the Mass.

Good words need good delivery (D 37). Even Shakespeare's poetry is meaningless if spoken too quickly, mumbled incomprehensibly, delivered in a sing-song 'parsonic' voice. This is even more important for children than for adults, because at least the latter are able to make mental allowances for bad public speaking. Yet that is no excuse: the clergy in general have not made a happy transition from the silence of the Latin Mass to the need for understanding in the vernacular. Meanwhile the general public has become accustomed to the high standards of TV and radio. If a paid

actor can whip up enthusiasm to advertise a product he
secretly does not like, how much greater should be our conviction and enthusiasm when we preach Christ whom we
believe by faith?

Learning from children

Children are good teachers and there is nothing they can
teach the priest better than prayer. The simplicity, faith and
directness of the child at prayer is a model for us all. The
atmosphere of a children's Mass is often as prayerful as that of
any monastery. This should be encouraged by the priest who
will learn to recognise the right moment for silent or
spontaneous prayer, and how long it should continue (cf D
37).

We mention this under the general heading of preparation,
because no celebrant should ignore the spirituality of a
children's Mass. One can too easily fall into the error of
regarding the children's Mass as being of little value, and
therefore allowing one's preparation to become inadequate.
Nothing could be further from the truth. Upon these celebrations rest the spirituality and worship of a large proportion of tomorrow's adults.

3. THE ADULTS (D 24)

Celebrating a children's Mass does not mean excluding
adults. The children's teacher, or leader, will of course be
present, and it is often useful to enlist the aid of other adults.
Helping the children in this way contributes to a happier
and more peaceful celebration. It is difficult to imagine any
priest successfully celebrating a children's Mass without the
aid of one or more adults.

Children require to be led. The Mass is for them a strange
and 'grown-up' experience so that no matter how hard a
priest tries, no matter how many adaptations are made, they

need some guidance in this relatively unaccustomed situation. The work of adults at a children's Mass is a form of liturgical ministry - like the collectors and sidesmen at an adult Mass. The priest has the principal ministry at Mass but he needs the help of other adults to lead the children to understand what it is he is doing.

Including adults at a children's Mass also underlines a basic principle - the Mass is for all. It is the centre-point of the entire community, and it is good that the children realise this from the beginning. As children attend the adult Mass on Sunday, so adults may attend the children's Mass. It is the same Mass although celebrated in a different manner.

Attendance means participation. The grown-up may not be able to take part in all the actions and words of the Mass because many will be in the language and forms of young children. But he should participate in as many as possible by praying, singing, processing, and so forth.

Praying is particularly important. Unfortunately some helpers at children's Masses maintain a stoic passivity and do what they are required to do and no more. The children are quick to notice such an attitude. Conversely, they are quick to notice the one who prays, who treats the Mass with care and respect. This is just the sort of leadership children are looking for.

Naturally what we say here also excludes the adult helper who looks upon the children's Mass with amused indifference. Or, worse, the one who regards it as a sort of comedy show. The teacher should be on the watch for such people and gently dissuade them from attending, and seek help from other and more sympathetic helpers.

One personal note of this writer. Fortunately not common, but to be avoided at all costs, is the demonstration Mass. By this we mean a children's Mass celebrated for the benefit of interested adults. There is no harm in the presence of a *small* group of adults at a *normal* children's Mass so that they can gain experience for their own groups, parishes or schools. But the specially planned Mass attended by priests and teachers who outnumber the poor children 4 to 1 is doomed to failure from the start. It is unreal and is not the worship of the community actually present. It is difficult to understand how a group of Catholic priests and teachers can be mere spectators at a Mass: they should be celebrating. In the same way it is difficult to see how the children can behave naturally while a large group of grown-ups breathes down their necks.

Altogether different is the children's Mass celebrated with the children accompanied by their parents. An example is the Leaver's Mass: basically a classroom Mass celebrated by the top class of the primary school at a time when the parents can attend, usually the evening. The adaptations are designed to involve the children, but the parents are encouraged to join in also. It is not a demonstration Mass; it is a Mass of thanksgiving for the years spent in the school, and a Mass of intercession for God's help in the new school and in the years ahead. Because their children's education is their concern too, the parents are invited. Never does one of these Masses end without a parent saying, 'I never understood the Mass properly until today.'

We have already said something about the 'ministry of the adult helper'. There are other and more active ministries for adults. Instead of 'making do' and singing without accompaniment, a children's group is better off if a pianist, organist or other instrumentalist can be persuaded to help. Once again, preparation is essential, and, in this example, preparation with the children. The accompanist may not be used to the unfamiliar ways of the group Mass.

Similarly for readers. A well-delivered reading by a grown-up whom all can hear and understand is better than the incomprehensible stumbling of a small child. The older the child the less this will be needed. And a child reader should not be excluded simply because he or she is more trouble to prepare.

In most cases the teacher, or group organiser, will be the only adult present apart from the priest. She plays an important part not only in the preparation of the Mass but also in its celebration. Some Masses are successful from the moment the priest arrives, and the teacher can take a back seat. More often, however, the children require positive leadership from teacher as well as priest. The 'leading', the interjected comments, ought to be given careful thought before the Mass. It helps to plan them with the priest so that they are made at the correct liturgical moment and do not interrupt the flow of the liturgy. The priest himself might have comments to make, in which case the two might be combined. Whatever is done, the aim is to lead the children easily and without fuss from one part of the celebration to another.

Nearly always we think of the priest as the only person with the power to preach. What, though, if he lack the ability to preach to children? The Directory (D 24) is in no two minds about it: some other adult may take over.

Preaching to children is no easy matter. Simple thoughts in simple language are essential. Not every priest is capable of this, and many know it. In which case they should have no compunction in handing over the task to someone who knows the children, their ideas and their language. It is more important that the children hear the Word of God clearly explained than that the priest maintain his 'position'.

The permission of the parish priest is required for a lay adult to preach to children. The reason is simple: the Mass may take place in a public church and the parish priest must make a judgement about the fittingness of the practice – others might be scandalised. In addition, the parish priest has the bishop's commission to preach the Word of God in a particular area. It is his duty to ensure that others who help him in this commission are suitable and know what they are about. But 'suitability' does not imply the choice of a man rather than a woman. The Directory makes no distinction; it would be surprising if it did because a much greater number of women than men teach the age-group of children we are considering.

No matter how good at speaking to children a priest may be, it may in any case be preferable sometimes that the teacher take over the preacher's role. This would apply in cases where the theme had been prepared so well by children and teacher beforehand that the priest's words might complicate the idea in the young minds. However, we must guard against making of the priest a mere sacrament-machine, and that is a real danger here.

The lay preacher should prepare well. Clarity, directness, brevity, dialogue are the foundations of the homily for children. We will discuss this at greater length when we go through the parts of the Mass. A good teacher will have no difficulties in preaching, particularly to her own class.

4. WHERE (D 25)

The place where a children's Mass is to be celebrated should be chosen with care. We began this chapter with the presumption heavily in favour of the classroom; that presumption can be applied also to the den of a scout troop, or any similar room for similar organisations. But a presumption is not a principle, and therefore we will examine this issue in more detail.

The Directory (D 25) states clearly that 'the church is the primary place'. After all, that is precisely what a church is built for. It is the place where the local community assembles to hear the Word of God and receive the Bread of Life. Within its walls the community is recognised as the Church as in no other place. Even when it is empty it is a sign of the living Church to all who pass by.

The church is a good place for school Masses when maybe two or three hundred children celebrate together. Apart from utilitarian considerations, the use of the local church can be a good lesson for the children in making them familiar with the building and in helping them recognise the church as important in the life of each parochial group. Every school should celebrate the Mass in the local church at least once or twice a term; it creates a real unity throughout the school.

However, big groups are not good for the celebration of children's Masses (D 28). Sheer size is a difficulty in itself: participation is increasingly difficult, the larger the group. The natural response and individual involvement envisaged by the Directory can take place only in small groups of twenty, thirty or, at the most, forty. Therefore the normal celebration of a children's Mass will involve a small group.

The small group does not rule out the use of the church. One solution is to seat the children in the sanctuary and allow them to stand close to the altar during the Eucharistic Prayer and communion. Such an experience will be useful at least once in a child's school life. Another solution is to adapt a side-chapel or some special corner of the church; many new churches have a 'day' chapel well-suited for this purpose. What will not do is familiar sanctuary-rails-pews arrangement of the average church. The building was designed for a far larger group, and children feel dwarfed by it. The priest seems to them too far away and 'mysterious'. (Incidentally it would be helpful to adults if some churches celebrated weekday Masses in a smaller chapel: ten people scattered among the pews of a five hundred seat church have little incentive to participate and feel at home.)

Two things are at stake: the dignity of the eucharist and the lively participation of the children. Dignity does not demand the use of the church; Pope Paul VI's example and that of thousands of bishops and priests is proof enough. Dignity is a relative factor which depends upon the interior attitude of the worshippers. Therefore if dignity is guaranteed, the telling factor is the lively participation of the children.

Without doubt, participation is better in familiar and comfortable surroundings. A classroom, or similar convenient room, enables the children to feel relaxed and at ease. With all unnecessary tensions eliminated they are free to express their participation and to concentrate more fully upon the action of the Mass (cf GI 253).

The Directory encourages the decoration by the children of the place of celebration (D 29). Some churches lend themselves to this sort of thing, in others it would be impossible. And impossibility includes not merely trying to brighten up a vast cavern of a church, but also the transport of materials and 'decorating' children from school to church. Far easier to decorate the walls of a classroom where the project can develop gradually and carefully.

There is one further reason why the Mass should be celebrated in a classroom - Christ is there. The class of children is a praying community and we have Christ's own promise that he will be with such a group. More than that, the children are engaged upon a process of discovery about God's world. Each new fact, each new discovery is not so much about the merely material world but about the creative love of the Father. The Mass is the summit of that love of God; it draws together the whole work of creation and of salvation and offers perfect thanksgiving to the Father. The Mass is the completion of the educational life of each child. What better place to complete that educational life than in the very place where it is lived - the classroom?

Celebrating Mass in a classroom does not mean making do with dust and dirt, or transforming the room into a miniature cathedral. Tidiness, cleanliness, the convenient arrangement of chairs etc. are all part of participation (cf D 29). On the other hand, it is not necessary to put carpets on the floor and hang curtains over the blackboard in an attempt to disguise the room. The Mass itself will draw together all the blemishes and all the decorations, all the failures and all the successes, all the sorrows and all the joys and make of them a thanksgiving sacrifice united with that of Christ himself.

6. WHEN

The educational system and family life dictate that most children's Masses will be celebrated on weekdays (D 20, cf D 27). But the weekend also has possibilities; in addition to the occasional Sunday Mass in the parish church, we can add special group occasions, such as an outing, scouts, First Communions, etc.

In the same way, the time of day selected depends upon the general time-table. If a school programme becomes congested, would-be celebrants should be wary of arranging a Mass at a time when the children are coming to, or going from school. It is better to cancel a Mass than to cause havoc at home and at school. In any case, early morning and late afternoon are bad times for children (not to mention school staff).

Important also is the frequency of children's Masses. Let us not forget that this form of the Mass is intended to lead the child to participation in the adult Mass (D 21), therefore the adult Mass should be more frequent in the life of the child. However frequency is often decided by other factors, the chief one being the availability of the priest. Taking an average size school (say ten classes) in an average length term (ten to thirteen weeks) there will be little opportunity for a classroom Mass more than once per class per term. We should also remember that there will almost certainly be one or two general Masses each term for the entire school. This adds up to about one Mass somewhere in the school each week. Few priests can deal with more than one each week: preparation suffers if he attempts more. Two per week would be absolute maximum. In most areas, one priest has to care for the entire school.

One Mass per class per term assists thorough preparation. This applies especially in cases where the preparation is the actual classroom work (as suggested earlier pp. 81ff.). The effort and expectancy put into the one celebration is difficult to reproduce more than once a term. Such restriction is no hardship, particularly if other liturgical celebrations are a feature of the life of the children (cf D 27 and chapter 3). The Mass should be the culmination of a series of non-eucharistic liturgies and therefore not need to be so frequent.

The Directory makes a passing reference to boarding schools (D 27). Its suggestion that Masses in these institutions should not be daily is sound common sense. Those who have experienced the life of compulsory daily Mass know the relative ineffectuality of that practice in the lives of children. The desire to attend Mass should be produced by other and more lasting means.

7. VISUAL AIDS (D 35 and 36)

Children are 'sensory motors', which is a technical way of saying that until they are about ten or eleven they live mostly through their physical senses. Thought, as a way of creating *ideas*, is only gradually arrived at. Children, in primary school, are interested in action more than in thought, which is why they become bored even during the most stimulating adult sermon - they need action for comprehension. Even adults are like that, though to a very much lesser degree. For that reason the liturgy is not just preaching and prayers. It uses colour, movement, sound and symbols to teach the truths of the faith. Vestment colours tell us something about the feast or season; water tells us of new life in baptism; the crucifix tells us about the sacrifice of Christ, and so on, right through the liturgy. Play these things down, or omit them altogether, and the liturgy becomes a barren wasteland of disembodied ideas - in fact, ceases to be liturgy. It has been said that the newly reformed liturgy has been reduced to that arid state; that is not the fault of the new liturgy but of individuals who have interpreted the new liturgy wrongly.

At Children's Masses the visual element demands greater emphasis; the almost hidden signs need to be more clearly seen. That is why we have already emphasised such things as the bread to be used at Mass, the way it can be seen on the altar, the vestments etc. Examples of other elements that might lend themselves to more emphasis are the crucifix in Lent, candles after Easter or on the feast of the Presentation of the Lord, hands raised in prayer at the 'Our Father', the book of readings. In other words, make sure that the signs and symbols of the liturgy are being seen and experienced by the children.

When we are sure the 'official' sensory elements are being experienced we can introduce some of the children's own. Decorating the place of celebration is one way - posters, cut out pictures, models associated with the Mass theme are other examples. Later we will see the possibilities of drama. All these visual aids have the great advantage of being the children's own creation and therefore doubly interesting for them: there is a feeling of identity which is not always present in adult-engineered situations.

Not that that should rule out altogether contributions from adults: adults have more technical skill to contribute. Examples include special lighting effects (for instance a spotlight on the book at the Gospel), professional posters, the use of slides and film.

The mere mention of slides and film is enough to send shivers up some spines. And yet why not? In days gone by (and today, when we can afford it) the church revelled in those colour slides we call stained glass, and the paintings around the walls of many a medieval church were about as close to a film as our forebears could get. Statues still dominate many a sanctuary.

The intelligent and restrained use of photography can produce a deep impact upon children, as we already know from the influence of TV. A short film (say, two or three minutes) illustrating the work of Mother Teresa of Calcutta would be ideal following the reading of the Good Samaritan parable followed in its turn by a dialogue of children with the celebrant on how to put the Gospel message into practice in their own lives. Slides are available depicting various biblical figures or scenes - used during the reading of a relevant section from the bible, these would have a good educative effect upon the children.

Drawbacks are obvious. The liturgy is not a film show. If it is used, film must serve the liturgy. Most of all, participation should not be sacrificed for the sake of film or slides; children should not be mere 'receivers' at Mass - they must give as well. The mute immovability of some children before the TV screen should act as a warning to the over-enthusiastic film-user. Short, sharp sequences, or just two or three colour slides, are enough to create an image in the mind, but not to divert interest and involvement in the things that really count.

Chapter 7

COME:
from the Entrance Song to the Opening Prayer

Children are special. They are certainly not just small-sized adults. At the same time they are but one part of the community we call the Church, the Mystical Body of Christ. The centre of that Body is the Mass in which the unity of the Mystical Body is sealed in the sacramental Body and Blood of Christ, offered to the Father in perpetual sacrifice. Any adaptation of the Mass must respect its basic structure because any change of that structure would be an axe to the root of community. The Directory tells us clearly what that structure is (D 38):

> Introductory Rites
> Liturgy of the Word
> Liturgy of the Eucharist
> Concluding Rite

Why is this structure essential and why must it never be altered? Because in the Liturgy of the Word 'God speaks to his people and Christ is still proclaiming his gospel' (CL 33). Scripture is inspired and in it we have God's own guarantee that he still speaks to us. Moreover, scripture, the bible, is God's voice speaking to his people, which is the Church; and the Church is never more real than when it is assembled for the Mass. The bible belongs to the Mass.

The bible is God's voice calling us, inviting us ('Repent, the kingdom of heaven is at hand'). An invitation demands a response. Our response stands no hope of reaching the Father unless we have a mediator, a go-between. Christ is that go-between by the offering of his Body and Blood in the Mass. The Liturgy of the Eucharist is therefore our response. And that is why Word and Eucharist constitute the two essential parts of the Mass: they are invitation and response - the history of salvation in miniature.

The invitation is made to a People, a community. So it follows that forming that community and preparing it to listen to God's Word is important - hence the Introductory Rites as part of the Mass's unchanging structure. Finally, response leads to witness. When the apostles had responded to Christ and had committed themselves to him, they were sent out to preach to all nations. The Concluding Rite is the sending-out of today's apostles.

The different parts of the Mass can be summed up in five 'commandments', or imperatives:

Come!
Listen!
Give thanks!
Take and eat!
Go!

Here we have the basis of the teaching on the Mass for children. So we will use these five imperatives as the five principal sections of our description of the children's Mass. But before doing so, there is one further point.

The Directory is anxious that there should not be too great a difference between children's Mass and adult Masses, and we have seen why (D 21). The Mass may on some occasions be so adapted that although adults can see the underlying identity, the children cannot. To help the children identify both forms of the Mass, and to help them to participate in the adult's Mass, the Directory lays it down that the following texts must remain unchanged in both children's and adult Masses (D 39):

> acclamations and responses to the priest's greeting
> the Lord's Prayer
> the Trinitarian formula at the final blessing.

The acclamations and responses are such phrases as 'And also with you', 'Praise to you, Lord Jesus Christ', etc. The selection of these responses for special attention is clear enough from the General Instruction on the Roman Missal 15, where they are referred to as the 'minimum of active participation'. Later in the same paragraph we read 'at least this much active participation is required to express and to foster the unity of communal action'. These responses and acclamations are the basic requirements for communal participation; they should be second nature to children so that they will see every Mass, adapted or not, as the Mass of the entire community. Introducing adapted versions into the children's Mass would possibly hold back children's participation at adult Masses, and inevitably result in the children becoming confused by mistakenly using their own versions at the adult Mass or vice versa.

For much the same reason the Lord's Prayer is to stay always in its present liturgical form. Such a fundamental prayer demands unanimity. The trinitarian formula at the conclusion of the Mass ('. . . in the name of the Father and of the Son and of the Holy Spirit') is important because it sums up the fact that the Mass is the action of the whole Trinity - through Christ, in the unity of the Spirit, to the honour of the Father. It is all too easy to forget this truth.

Finally the Directory singles out the Creed for special comment (D 39). This Profession of Faith is a somewhat different case from those we have been considering; it will be discussed more fully in its chronological place in the Mass, later in this chapter.

COME

Aim

To make a listening community (GI 24 and D 40). Community means 'being one', therefore children, teacher and priest should feel a common purpose, should be aware of the Christ who is with all and in all. Furthermore this community should be a listening one; that is to say, one which waits expectantly to hear the Word of God, not simply because it is a colourful story, but because the life of the community will be changed by it. God has something to say to his People, and they are waiting for that Word.

Community cannot be formed without comfortable seating. Discomfort makes one think too much of oneself: others are ignored. So the room, its heating, lighting, ventilation, seating are all-important. Difficult too is forming community out of people who do not know each other, though that is what has to be done at most Sunday Masses. Children in particular should already know each other and be accustomed to each other's habits.

Forming the 'listening community' should be simple and straightforward (D 40). Too many actions and too many words obscure the real issue. This, of course, is applicable to the entire Mass. There is the constant danger of being swept away by an unending wave of bright ideas. The children may be excited by each novelty but meanwhile they are missing the point of the celebration. The Directory, aware of this danger, allows the priest to cut down the number of parts of the Introductory Rites. Here is the full list of the parts:

Entrance Song
Greeting
Introduction
Penitential Rite
'Lord have mercy'
'Glory to God in the highest'
Opening Prayer

Of these, a Children's Mass must always contain at least the Opening Prayer *preceded* by one of the other parts (D 40). Under normal circumstances the choice will be between the Penitential Rite, 'Lord have mercy' and 'Glory be', because it is difficult to see how a Mass for children can begin without some form of Entrance Song, a greeting, and an introduction. Omitting one or more parts of the Introductory Rites gives the opportunity to concentrate upon another part and perhaps amplify it. However, the changes should be rung frequently so that all the parts may be used at one time or another.

1. *Entry* (D 40)
The first job is to get the children together as a community. That may present no difficulty if, as in the case of classroom Masses, the children have already been in the room for some time. But if the Mass comes at the end of a long period of work in the classroom the children may be restive and in need of a break. Therefore, church or classroom, the getting together of the community can be performed in any one of several ways. All of these methods make use of some form of procession because that is one of the easiest ways of gathering a community together (D 34). The solemnity of a processional walk and the act of moving from one place to another give the entry procession the edge over other methods.

a. The procession of the priest, vested, into the room – the normal method of commencing any Mass in a church. It has the advantage (in classroom as well as church) of creating an air of expectancy.

b. Procession of priest with children. This is better because it involves all the children in movement instead of merely in waiting for the priest. The children are part of the action.

c. Priest meets the children outside (e.g. in the playground), draws them together with a few words, perhaps begins a hymn and leads them to the place of celebration. This is a variant of b. above. The advantage lies in the transition of mood: this gives added solemnity to the occasion. A disadvantage is that children who have been running around a playground usually need time to simmer down before such a solemn thing as the Mass.

d. The priest enters in street clothes with all he needs for Mass. Under his guidance the children prepare the altar and finally the priest vests, explaining the various items of liturgical dress. Although the entry procession is virtually non-existent this is the method which most priests will have to adopt through force of circumstances at the majority of classroom Masses. As often as possible he should try to vary this method by using one or other of those mentioned above.

There is much to be said for having the children prepare the altar at the Offertory (altar cloth, candles, chalice etc.) when, since the altar is about to be used for the first time at the Mass, its preparation is needed. When there is an adequate entry procession this could still be the case, if desired. However our problem here is the virtual lack of any procession. Preparing the altar at the beginning is a way of concentrating the children's minds upon the event of the

Mass. The hymn, or other music, comes when all the preparation is complete.

Choosing the Entry Song, or hymn, requires great care.
First of all it should be connected in some way with the
overall theme of the Mass because its function is to unite a
community physically and mentally. No matter what was
going on a few minutes before, the children are united in
song. Singing together demands working together. Singing the same words demands (hopefully) thinking the same
thoughts.

Song is not the only way of accompanying the Entry Rite -
instruments, either as a band or solo, and recorded music are
possibilities in place of song. However, they have the drawback either of involving only a few children, or of having
no words, or both.

Talking of song and procession leads naturally to *dance*.
The rhythm of the music and the rhythm of the procession of
children lend themselves to some form of expressive movement. A gay folk song executed to the steps of what appears
to be a funeral march will just not do. Children are masters
at putting music into action, and very many schools place
great importance upon the creative art of dance. Dance
within the liturgy is nothing new. Even the priest's own
ritual movements are really another form of dance.

If a large group of children is to express some aspect of
the Mass in dance form, careful planning and practice are
required. Better to have no music at all than to have chaos.
Much depends upon time and space availability but it should
be remembered that extravagant movements and great
spaces are not always necessary. The priest's liturgical gestures are a good example of expressive movement within a
confined space.

2. Greeting

Between the Entry and the Greeting there is often a lot of activity - hymn books being dropped and picked up again, searches for the music of the 'Lord have mercy', low-key squabbles about the possession of a seat, and so on. Therefore the priest should pause before uttering his first words, look round the group in a friendly and expectant fashion; in amazingly few seconds complete silence will descend. Everyone is ready.

The priest's first liturgical words are usually 'In the name of the Father . . .' How important these words are. They express one of the deepest theological insights granted to man. Do we say them with faith or with unthinking habit? The sign we make with the words is the sign of our Christianity: it is our badge. Or does it look as if we are trying to brush away a fly?

To the priest let us say this: begin as you mean to go on. Go on with reverence, with care, in prayerfulness; make each gesture count and, if the children are to make the gesture with you, lead them decisively and at a pace they can keep up with. Gestures such as the Sign of the Cross are adult yet simple, so they should be made not childishly but in an adult and mature fashion.

There are three standard formulas of the Greeting. Bearing in mind what was said about D 39, we consider these formulas as being amongst those acclamations and responses which should never be changed at a children's Mass. There is unlimited scope for variation immediately after.

Admittedly some of the phrases are difficult for young children - but if they are said by the priest with warmth, friendliness and conviction they will very soon get the idea. The gesture of the hands and arms is an open, ample and all-embracing one; the smile on the face of the priest confirms what the words have to say. Gestures must always match words.

In small groups individual greetings are possible. Children are delighted if the priest greets them by name and shakes them by the hand. But whatever is done, the Greeting should be made as by a friend and father. The sincerity and warmth of those initial words often decide the mood of the rest of the celebration.

3. *Introduction*

No Mass should be without an Introduction. Through it the celebrant can focus the minds of his congregation upon one important aspect of the theme. Nearly always, the congregation at a children's Mass already knows the theme because it has been preparing it for some time. In that case it is the priest's task to relate the general theme to one specific religious point which can be traced in the prayers, readings and homily of the Mass. But the Introduction is not a homily. One simple idea, expressed in simple, straightforward language, is all that is required.

There are other ways of introducing the Mass. One of the children, reading from a prepared text, will command much attention. Children are fascinated to hear one of their own number playing such a prominent part in the celebration.

A short piece of film, or a couple of slides, or a large picture are useful at the Introduction. Not only do the children hear something but they see something as well; it is an old, well-proven educational ploy. Objects work as well as pictures. For instance, a Mass about justice and hunger might begin by the priest unveiling two meals on a tray - one the sort of meal any of the children present might expect to find on arriving home that evening, the other a meal of a starving child in the slums of Calcutta. Here again, brevity and simplicity are all-important.

4. *Penitential Rite*

Sin builds walls between us, it destroys community and brotherhood in Christ. Before celebrating the act which destroyed sin and united all people in Christ, the community confesses its sins and asks God's forgiveness: it removes the barriers which separate people. The Penitential Rite re-unites brothers before they join together in the family sacrificial meal.

How far this principle can be seen by children in the present Rite is not clear. The 'I confess' lacks the concreteness which children require for full comprehension (though it is not as bad as some of the appalling Acts of Contrition children used to be made to learn before First Confession: they taxed the understanding even of adults). The third form of the Penitential Rite is more hopeful because it is freely adaptable.

Any custom-made Penitential Rite for children should be short and related to the theme of the whole Mass. There is no time for children to think deeply about the words, to work out their meaning; the meaning should be clear immediately. Here is an example from a Mass on Feeding the Hungry:

We are sorry for when we have been greedy. Lord, have mercy.
We are sorry for not sharing our sweets and things with our friends. Christ, have mercy.
We are sorry for wasting so much food. Lord, have mercy.

Admittedly this example makes no mention of the real theological issue - that all things come from God and man must share with all, or take responsibility for those who are starving. But such ideas are too cerebral for most under-elevens. It is the function of other parts of the Mass to touch upon those ideas, particularly at the Offertory and Eucharistic Prayer. More important at the beginning of the Mass is something direct and concrete which the children can understand immediately.

An alternative method is for the priest to help the children in an examination of conscience. A series of direct questions leads each child to consider in silence his own conduct and then express his sorrow aloud by 'Lord, have mercy', or 'Jesus, I am sorry'. Here a few examples to fit in the theme of charity:

Priest: Do you answer back your mother and father?
    (Pause in silence).
Priest: Jesus, we are sorry.
Children: Jesus, we are sorry.

Priest: Do you sometimes refuse to share your toys with your brothers and sisters?
    (Pause in silence).
Priest: Lord, have mercy.
Children: Lord, have mercy.

Priest: Do you lose your temper and fight in the playground?
    (Pause in silence).
Priest: Lord, forgive us.
Children: Lord, forgive us.

Then follows the Absolution, or Reconciliation. The standard formula, 'May almighty God have mercy on us, forgive us our sins . . .' is without doubt too difficult for many children, but not all. Spoken slowly and with conviction, most children will understand at least the main idea. Some authors suggest a re-wording of the Absolution: 'May God be good to us, forgive us all that we have done wrong, and one day make us happy with him in our home in heaven.'

Because sin destroys community what better thing than that the children should now express their reconciliation? The very young ones would not think twice about kissing each other, but a handshake would be more suitable for the older child. There is no conflict here with the Sign of Peace before Communion: one sign establishes unity before listening to the Word, the other re-affirms that unity before receiving the Word at communion.

The priest does not have to lead the Penitential Rite himself (cf GI 29). Conducted by a child the Rite may escape the danger of appearing to be a grown-up's subtle way of 'telling-off' the children. It also provides another chance of individual participation.

Occasionally the Penitential Rite is more effective after the readings, especially if the Mass is of a penitential character. Instead of the Rite preparing for the readings, the readings prepare for the act of penance. After a reading on man's weakness and God's love (e.g. Prodigal Son) the Penitential Rite would come as the natural climax, as an inevitable call to the Father for forgiveness.

5. *'Lord, have mercy'*
Some people find it difficult to deal with the 'Lord, have mercy': it seems to be neither properly penitential, nor fully a litany of praise. Certain it is that it has found its present place and meaning in the Mass only through historical accident. The new Roman Missal makes it clear that the 'Lord, have mercy' is a rounding off of the Penitential Rite. Indeed it is an integral part of the third Rite.

But it can be viewed from a different perspective. Young children cannot stand much of being 'spoken at'. They have an extremely limited capacity of what they can comprehend through the spoken word. To maintain their attention and interest they need frequent bursts of song or some form of acclamation. The 'Lord, have mercy' fits the bill very well. It is simple and repetitive, therefore the music can be learned easily. And if there is to be no 'Gloria' then it is a good song break between the wordiness of the Penitential Rite and the even longer talk of the Liturgy of the Word.

For the ambitious there is a further possibility. Tropes. These are 'brief text-insertions' (GI 30) with the 'Lord, have mercy'. They were once very popular with our medieval forebears and could have a number of advantages if used at children's Masses. First, a trope can break up the monotony of the repetitive text. Second, the 'Lord, have mercy' can be designed for a particular theme (as it already is in the third Penitential Rite). Third, it can add an extra touch of solemnity to a special occasion.

Here are some examples:

Theme - Dependence on God:
Lord, maker of the world, have mercy.
Christ, who saved us from sin, have mercy.
Lord, our Father in heaven, have mercy.

Theme - First Communion:
Lord, who have given us this lovely day, have mercy.
Christ, so that we may be ready for you, have mercy.
Lord, we want to be more like Jesus, have mercy.

Set to music, these tropes would probably sound better than when spoken. Alternatively, the first part can be spoken by a soloist and the children reply, in speech or in song, 'have mercy'.

6. *'Glory to God in the highest'*

A magnificent hymn of praise, full of joy, full of life - but not so easy to sing, less easy for youngsters to understand. Yet understanding is not everything. A group of children able to sing two or three musical versions of this hymn may well prove to be the basis a parish needs to teach it to the adults. The priest who is striving to build up a good sung Sunday liturgy should not forget the help he can obtain from the local schools.

Yet the fact remains that the Roman Calendar does not often require the use of the 'Glory to God' on those days when children's Masses are likely to be celebrated. That does not mean it must be omitted if it is not obligatory. A rousing cheerful piece of sung praise may be just the thing before the readings. To help composers, the Directory allows changes in the official text (D 31). Such changes are often minor ones and hardly noticeable. What about something more radical? Here is an example from a private French source:

> Father, we give you glory because of your great love for everyone:
>> through Jesus Christ, our Lord. Amen.
>
> We give you glory because you send the Word who is our Light:
>> through Jesus Christ, our Lord. Amen.
>
> We give you glory because you give us the Holy Spirit who makes our hearts strong:
>> through Jesus Christ, our Lord. Amen.
>
> Listen today to our prayer, full of joy and confidence:
>> through Jesus Christ, our Lord. Amen.
>
> Make us grow in your love and in the love of our brothers:
>> through Jesus Christ, our Lord. Amen.

A musical version might allow for a soloist singing the first part of each stanza, the rest of the group joining in 'through Jesus Christ, our Lord. Amen.'

Of a completely different character in this Malaysian example (private source):

'Glory to God in heaven and peace to his people on earth. We praise you, we adore you, we thank you, holy God. Amen.'

7. Opening Prayer D 50, D 51 (also Prayer over the Offerings and Prayer after Communion)

The Opening Prayer is a short and snappy prayer. So short that it is often rushed through and is finished before you know what is happening. Yet the Opening Prayer is the first great prayer of the Mass; after all the preliminaries it is the first moment you can say that the community is really and truly united. It is the worshipping Church's first major prayer together.

It is often called 'Collect' because the priest gathers together the intentions of the whole assembly and sums them up in one, all-embracing prayer (GI 32). This is clearer if the celebrant does what the Roman Missal recommends (it is more than a recommendation: the Missal presumes that it will be done): that is, a pause for silent prayer after the invitation 'Let us pray'. Only after a few moments during which everybody has the chance of offering a silent, personal prayer should the priest recite aloud the official text.

Silence is an essential part of the new liturgy. That is a fact emphasised repeatedly in the documents of the Church - Constitution on the Sacred Liturgy 30; Instruction on Sacred Music 17; General Instruction on the Roman Missal 23; Directory of Masses with Children 22, 37, 46. Much opposition to the reformed liturgy would evaporate if celebrants were more conscious of this.

To help the congregation, particularly children, use the silent pause profitably the celebrant may suggest a theme for the silent prayer at the Opening Prayer. For example, the Opening Prayer of the Epiphany might begin: 'Let us pray that we shall see God face to face.' There follows the silent pause, then the priest recites the Opening Prayer which is an amplification of the invitation. The invitation must provide a direct link with the theme of the Opening Prayer.

If the Opening Prayer is to sum up the prayer of all the children, one thing is clear. It must be about ideas and in words which children can understand (D 50). The English translation of the Directory uses the phrase, 'the priest has to remain in touch with the children': that expresses it perfectly.

So that he can keep in touch, the priest is permitted to choose any prayers from the Roman Missal (here we are also considering the Prayer over the Offerings and the Prayer after Communion). As long as he respects the liturgical season (a Mass in honour of our Lady celebrated on Easter Sunday is the sort of thing to be avoided) the priest has a vast choice. However, the choice is of themes, not of words. While many of the themes of the Missal's Opening Prayers may be applicable to children, the words are by and large unsuitable.

Again, the Directory to the rescue (D 51). Adaptation of the prayers to the needs of children is recommended. But notice that this means adapatation of pre-existing Missal prayers, not the composition of totally new ones. Why? Because composing Opening Prayers is an art not given to many. They constitute an art form in themselves and the unwary dabbler often falls into the trap of moralising and childishness warned against by the Directory.

Fortunately that does not rule out new Opening Prayers altogether. Bishops can, and already have in some cases, approve the publication of new texts. These new prayers are especially important when 'theme Masses' are being discussed, because many themes of interest to children (e.g. new term, new baby in the family) are not to be found in the Missal in the way children understand them. Carefully written prayers to match specially selected Readings do much to create an intelligible and integrated liturgy.

Let us consider the guide-lines both for adapting pre-existing prayers for children, for which the permission of the bishop is not required, and for composing new texts under the auspices of a bishop:

a. The prayer must speak of the concrete situation of *this* assembly. The forming of theoretical ideas is beyond most children before they reach ten or eleven; even then it is sketchy. To say, 'thank you, God, for helping Johnny Smith get better' is far preferable to 'we thank you, for the graces you bestow upon those who love you'. Children need to know precisely what those graces are.

b. The prayer should have only one central idea. Too many ideas lead to confusion and in the end nobody prays but the priest. 'Thank you, God, for helping Johnny Smith get better, for giving us good weather, for allowing us to have a nice outing to the seaside and for taking our pet hamster up to heaven' (sic) - that is an all-too-common mess.

c. Most prayers follow a classical formula: the statement of a gift or an attribute of God followed by a relevant petition or thanksgiving. For example: 'God our Father, you often made sick people get better through the power of your Son, Jesus (statement). We thank you for helping Johnny Smith get better: through Christ our Lord . . .'
The Prayer over the Gifts and the Prayer after Communion should normally follow that pattern.

d. The prayer should be in the language of children without being childish. The Opening Prayer is a peak. All that goes before it is working up to it. It is a high point in the prayer of the children's community. Yet it is not a solitary peak. It is like the first of a range of higher mountains. The next, one of the highest, is the Liturgy of the Word.

Chapter 8

LISTEN:
the Liturgy of the Word

The 'Amen' resounds. The Opening Prayer is over and there is a coughing, a murmuring, a rustling of paper and a scraping of chairs. Then all . . .

LISTEN

Aim

To hear God speaking to us now. Christ 'is present in his word, since it is he himself who speaks when the holy scriptures are read in the church' (CL 7). 'For in the liturgy God speaks to his people and Christ is still proclaiming his gospel' (CL 33).

This is not to deny that scripture is difficult for young children. Even the apostles could not understand all Christ's words at first; they needed explanation. Scripture, difficult or not, is the living voice of God and the liturgy is its most natural setting. And because it is a living voice we should be aware that God gives the grace of comprehension to his hearers. Not that we are advocating some sort of divine magic which renders the most incomprehensible passage crystal clear: scripture scholars would be out of business if we were. What we do say is that the Word is a seed and if the children listen in faith and are helped by the adults that seed will take root in their hearts (cf D 41).

'Helped by the adults.' There lies our task. To fulfil that task we, priests and laity, need to be imbued with scripture.

We cannot hand on what we have not got. That does not mean that we must be scholars, able to wrestle with the knotty problems of exegesis. But it does mean that we should become familiar with the bible, should love it and treasure it. It does not take much to fall in love with the bible; a daily chapter of the Old Testament and two of the New is enough to make it happen.

The love we have of scripture we should pass on to the children in our charge (cf D 47). So many otherwise intelligent children leave school intellectually defenceless in matters of faith. Learning at school is one thing, but living the faith in the world is another. A love of scripture and a constant reading of it will not provide easy 'answers' to problems, but it will continue a process of religious maturation. The child who continues throughout childhood reading the Word of God in faith is one who will live by that Word, love by that Word, hope because of it and pray a prayer fed by it.

I. THE READINGS

a. *How many?* (D 42)

Our aim is that the listening child should take from the Liturgy of the Word at least one clear message. Some children can take more than one such message: usually this depends on age. Even if there are two readings with but one theme it may still be that younger children will become confused under the sheer weight of words. Therefore at Masses with pre-First Communion children it is advisable to have only one reading.

The older child (from about seven years of age upwards) is capable of more. With help from priest and teacher he can begin to understand the similarity of theme between some Old Testament passages and a Gospel. Also his ability to listen and to make judgements is increasing rapidly - a skill much concentrated upon in the primary school. From a training point of view it is advisable for the child to become accustomed to two readings, because on most Sundays he will be subjected to three. Meanwhile the single reading should not be ruled out altogether; circumstances may sometimes suggest it.

It need hardly be said that three readings for any child under twelve is far too much. It would be interesting to know at what age so many readings become comprehensible and acceptable to the average child. Sixteen perhaps?

The gospel reading is the sine qua non of the Liturgy of the Word: it may never be omitted. The reason is simple: not only is the gospel the Word of God but it is about the incarnate Word of God, Jesus Christ, our Lord. All scripture is an account of God's interventions in the history of man. But the Gospel tells us of the ultimate intervention, of the greatest of all God's saving acts. Christ is the Way, the Truth and the Life. Therefore we should always listen to his words and his actions.

D 42 is a strange paragraph because the first sentence lays it down that regarding the number of readings we should follow the rules of the episcopal conference; the second sentence in effect says we need not follow these rules if the readings are difficult. What is more, the first sentence speaks of the readings of Sundays and feasts, the second of Sundays and weekdays. Why the omission of feasts in the second sentence? (N.B. Some translators, apparently confused by this, have translated the second sentence as 'Sundays or feasts'. That makes more sense but is not a correct translation of the original Latin.) In all of this there is a rather vague reference to the powers which espiscopal conferences have to reduce the number of readings on feast days from three to two for pastoral reasons. As far as children's Masses are concerned the principle is clear: the number of readings may be reduced from three to two, or from two to one, whenever this is judged necessary by those who are in charge of the children.

b. *Where from?* (D 43)
In paragraphs 41 to 48 the Directory has one aim for children: to listen to *and* comprehend God's Word. If the children cannot comprehend the official Lectionary reading for the day then any other Lectionary reading may be chosen, or any suitable reading from the bible.

Do not be legalistic in choosing readings. The compilers of the Directory do not expect the organiser of a children's Mass to hunt through the thousands of readings in the Lectionary when all the time he knows of a bible passage which will suit his purpose exactly. In any case, most bible readings comprehensible to children can be found in the Lectionary - but it is usually easier to find them in the bible.

Comprehension, or understanding, should be taken in a wide sense. Comprehension is not only understanding what the passage means, but also understanding how it relates to this particular celebration today. For example, a reading about the baptism of Jesus would be incomprehensible at a First Communion Mass, even if the reading itself is clear enough. Comprehension involves the complete context in which a reading is proclaimed.

On major feast days this is usually no problem: the whole Mass is directed to one theme and all the prayers and readings of the official text have been chosen with the theme in mind. Not so on ordinary weekdays. During the greater part of the year the prayers and the readings are unrelated: the prayers come from the previous Sunday, or are of a saint, while the readings follow a continuous cycle which has nothing to do with Sunday or saint. And that is fine for the daily Mass-goer who follows the readings day by day, but not for the child whose Mass is occasional.

All this points to one thing - the theme Mass. We have already said something about the growth of a celebration from the ordinary life of the children. A theme Mass is one in which prayers, readings and whatever can be adapted are chosen to express the one idea of that celebration. Ordinary life is seen as part of the Mass, and the Mass as part of life. A Mass well-planned around one idea or theme can do much to aid the understanding of children.

Planning a theme Mass is not easy. A teacher's familiarity with the bible may not be sufficient for discovering suitable readings. Priests also find it difficult. Hence the Directory's recommendation that bishops' conferences should compile children's lectionaries. Many countries have already done so, England and Wales included (*Mass for Young People*, St Paul's Press, 1973). However, the Directory obliges no one to use these lectionaries. Not only is choosing from the bible a permissible way of producing readings, but so also is the use of other lectionaries compiled by individuals or groups. There are many of these which have been compiled with limited-range age groups in mind; they are more useful than those which have children of indeterminate age in mind. A teacher will soon discover the lectionary particularly suited to her class, and that, coupled with a sensible use of the bible, should help the children to hear and understand God's message.

c. *Simplified versions of scripture* (D 43, 44, 45)
To cut down the number of readings may not be enough. In any case, quantity or length is not necessarily a bad thing. A too-short reading might defeat its own purpose by being finished so quickly that the children will have had no time

to 'tune in' to it. This can happen even with adults; some of the Gospel readings of the new Lectionary are over before most people realise they have begun. It is a common failing to assume that because a scripture passage is short it must therefore be crystal clear. Comprehension is assisted by much of what we might be tempted to term as 'padding'. Jesus realised this; consequently many of his teachings were couched in the form of a parable.

More problematical is the question of simplification. Scripture was written by adults for adults. The words and ideas are very often too difficult for the young child. The problem is to help the child understand something of what the particular passage has to say without destroying its identity as a piece of divinely inspired writing. We must always bear in mind that we are dealing with a form of writing quite unlike any other: God as well as man is the author.

Simplification is often necessary. How far can you go before the scripture ceases to be scripture and becomes the re-telling of a scripture story? There is no answer to that question without consideration of the actual passage. Certainly to change the literary form of a scriptural passage is unacceptable. For example, to change a passage of St Paul's first Letter to the Corinthians into a story about the sinfulness of Corinth would be a change in literary form.

Likewise paraphrase is not an acceptable form of simplification for liturgical purposes. Many of the children's versions now on sale are of this type. We must respect the structure and form of scripture as well as its content. But judgement upon particular examples is usually very difficult and even experts cannot always agree.

Surprising though it may seem, simplification of scripture is nearly always better done by the children's teacher. Only she knows the mental and verbal capacity of the children, and experience has shown that the balanced teacher produces a balanced simplification. It is not a question of re-writing scripture but of simplifying a word here, expanding a phrase there. The more complicated scriptural passages are not normally relevant to children's themes.

d. *Ways of reading*

The main aim is to get God's message across. Reading can make or mar that aim. Obviously reading is a major form of child participation but the ideal of participation should take second place to clarity. Therefore we should never be afraid to use adult readers when necessary (D 24). But only when necessary. In classes of seven year olds and upwards it should always be possible to find and train a competent reader.

There is more to the readings than reading. Taking a passage out of its original setting often makes it more difficult to understand, therefore a brief introduction by priest, teacher or even a child helps the understanding (D 47). The emphasis must be upon 'brief': this is not the place for a sermon or an exercise in exegesis. All that is required is a summary of the principal theme and its application to the lives of the children. The following example illustrates this: it is an introduction to the Gospel of the Prodigal Son:

'In this gospel Jesus teaches us that his Father is always ready to forgive our sins.'

But introductions do need preparation: the longest introduction is the unprepared one.

The Directory suggests that on saints' days the introduction might include a reference to the saint's life. Behind this is the important truth that a saint is a saint precisely because of his conformity to the gospel message. At the same time the saint is put before us as an example of what can be done, what we can do with God's grace.

More exciting than a solo reading is a *group reading*, like the script of a play. With different children taking the parts - narrator, Jesus, Mary, an apostle, etc. - a number of things happen: more children are involved, they have a better opportunity of learning the inner message of the reading, and the simplification of the language is easier. It should be noted that this method of reading applies equally to Old Testament, Epistle and Gospel. The Directory (D 47) makes it quite clear in its reference to the Holy Week Passion reading that reading the Gospel at a children's Mass is not the priest's inalienable prerogative.

Reading a script is only one step from full *drama*. That step should be taken. There is something in the nature of drama which demands our involvement, our commitment to a cause, like no other art form. We can sink into and become submerged by music, but drama forces us to make a judgement, to take a point of view. Children are more affected by drama than adults: watch them in front of the TV or at a school nativity play. Involved in a drama of the gospel, children are in an ideal learning situation; they become part of the action, part of the story, part of the proclamation of the Word. And that is what Christian education is all about.

Planned and rehearsed with care, a dramatic presentation of the Gospel message can be as beautiful for the adult as for the child taking part. It is important however that the gospel be adhered to; simplification there must be, but no adaptation which makes the drama more important than the gospel. Almost as important is the low key in which the drama should be performed; overdo it and the whole Mass will suffer. Performed with taste and discretion, it will leave a lasting imprint upon the minds of the children.

Close to drama is involvement in the *gospel procession* suggested by the Directory (D 34). To do this, much depends upon the space available: a procession must *go* somewhere to be of any significance. That significance lies in the dignity of God's Word and the honour shown to it by the worshippers. Carrying the gospel book in solemn procession has a way of showing the importance of the Word in the lives of us all, and if the children can take part, so much the better. If not all the children then perhaps three or four, representing the others, can solemnly carry the book for the priest - even hold it while he reads from it. Candles too are a dramatic way to underline the gospel's importance: either all the children holding a lighted candle (as at the Feast of the Presentation of the Lord) or a group of four (rather as at a Solemn Mass).

A reading has a way of coming alive when illustrated with *visual aids* - paintings, posters, montages, slides or film. We have already discussed the principle of using such aids. A class project on a parable such as the Prodigal Son could produce a number of paintings, each one depicting a major incident in the parable - leaving home, wasting the money, repentance, return home, the father's welcome. As the priest slowly reads the story two children hold up the appropriate painting in full sight of the others. This is really a technique employed by many a children's TV programme: sound and vision combine to stimulate the children's imagination.

Projected slides serve the same purpose although they have the drawback of not being something of the children's own creation. The same thing applies to a short film. In painting a picture the children have to consider the parable and let their imagination work on it long before the Mass takes place.

2. THE CHANT BETWEEN THE READINGS

Experience of the working of the reformed liturgy shows that the 'reading chants' deserve better treatment. They should not be too closely allied to the Entry, Offertory, Communion and Recessional music. The mood of the 'reading chants' is meditative: they are a reflection upon the readings and are a response-in-prayer to what has just been read. Hence the name 'Responsorial Psalm'. The other chants, or hymns, almost always accompany a procession, or at least an action, and do not have to be textually related to the action. For example, the St Patrick's Day hymn serves equally well as Entry or as Recessional, but would be utterly out of place after a reading.

Some hymns do fit the occasional reading. But there is nothing better than a well chosen psalm (cf D 46). The 150 psalms have the uncanny ability of being able always to provide the right prayer for the right occasion. Joy and sorrow, penance and jubilation, praise and petitition - they are all there. Whatever the reading, there seems to be a psalm to supply a prayerful comment.

Undoubtedly the psalms sometimes make difficult understanding for young children, but there are many which are crystal clear, or which can be adapted for the use of the younger congregation. Furthermore psalms have the distinct advantage of being able to be sung, verse by verse, by a soloist, with the congregation periodically joining in with a refrain. Using this technique a whole school can acquire a repertory of psalms in a remarkably short time. English-speaking Catholics are not renowned for their hymnology: a love of the psalms bred at school could be one way of setting the record straight.

A simple Alleluia verse is another solution, as the Directory suggests (D 46). As with the psalm, it should be related to the reading; possibly, however, in a slightly different way. The psalm is a prayerful comment on what has just been read: the Alleluia verse is an acclamation, a shout. Of course, in the adult form of the Mass, the Alleluia verse relates to the reading which *follows*, i.e. the Gospel. Need this always be so? We think not. It is easier to respond to what has just been heard than to anticipate what is still to be heard. Like many other things in the liturgy, a little flexibility here will not come amiss.

Sometimes simple silence is the best response. Mass can be a noisy affair, and with the best will in the world, coupled with the brightest theories about communal participation, the need for a little peace and quiet is understandable. Children need quiet just as much as adults - and indeed children are more at home with periods of community silence than are adults. Children get down to the job of thinking and praying; adults sit there wondering when the priest is going to get on with the Mass.

Participation does not only come about through word and action, though they undoubtedly are the major ways. Praying together in silence can be just as effective (cf D 22, 37, 46; CL 30; GI 23). But to make it work, some form of direction is necessary. Like the Opening Prayer, a brief word connecting the essential content of the reading with something the children feel in their own lives will help them think and pray a little.

3. THE HOMILY

The success of a children's Mass often depends upon the homily (cf D 48). Through it the children are led to see the connection between God's Word, the theme of the Mass, and their everyday lives. And not only the Word and the theme: the homily looks forward too, looks forward to the eucharist and its place in the lives of all men. The Mass is that which knits together the world of God and the world of man and makes them one; the homily makes the children conscious of this oneness.

Preaching to children is probably the most difficult part of the Mass. Other parts are simplifications of pre-existing texts, or, at the most, only the addition of a single comment or introduction. The homily must be original, fresh, and educational: that is a tall order for the priest, especially one who has not been trained as a teacher. Fortunately the Directory has opened the way for the lay-preacher at children's Masses (cf D 24 and our comments in Chapter 6): this will be of great help to the priest who feels he cannot speak to children at a comprehensible level.

But many priests give in without trying. It is surprising how many there are who assume that they have nothing to say to children; how many there are who are frightened at the prospect of dealing with thirty or forty youngsters. In some ways preaching to children calls for more care, and preparation, but the effort is always worthwhile. Their spontaneous and immediate reaction can be most gratifying. And as a side-product, the need to be simple and to the point is a great help towards the preparation of adult homilies. Most priests can talk to children, if only they would give themselves a chance.

The first and *indispensable* requirement is directness. The point of the homily should be obvious almost from the beginning. 'Working round to the point' is a good method of losing the children's attention, or at least getting them interested in peripheral and unimportant ideas. In any case, time is scarce: the homily should be relatively short. Remember, the children have already had to do a lot of listening and there is still much to come in the second half of the Mass. They have a limit to the amount they can take in.

Directness is served by interest. The preacher must create that interest in his (or her) first two or three sentences. How to do it? Children love stories about anything - about home, about the local football team, about their favourite TV pro-gramme, about almost anything. Whatever it is it should be to the point and not just a piece of 'padding': for example a tale about a naughty boy who continues to be naughty despite all his promises (true repentance), the leadership of the local football captain in leading his team to victory (Christ as our leader, and the importance of working together). Do they appear too simple? We must never for-get that all human virtues are but a participation in the divine. Religion is not about candles and incense, but about living.

Besides stories, pictures or objects (a stethoscope at a Mass for the sick) can capture the interest and imagination (cf D 36). Let us not forget what we said in Chapter 6 about visual aids. A simple method of creating interest in the homily is to show a picture which has some relationship to the gospel of Mass. First the children can be asked what they see, who is in the picture, what he is doing, what they would have done had they been there. The second stage is talking about what the children can actually do in order to put the gospel into practice. And on some occasions none of these things will be necessary because the preacher will be able to use the gospel to plunge straight into his subject. This method works best of all in the dialogue homily.

Dialogue is the spice of a good homily. When he speaks to the priest spontaneously, in his own words, the individual child comes alive; he relates to the theme of the homily in a way unlike any other. If called upon to answer a question or make a comment, something comes from the child which is uniquely his own. He has to think about what is being said and then articulate his thoughts; and that is a good learning process.

Even if he is not actually answering a question or making a comment, each child is more alive, more aware of what is going on when he listens to what his friends have to say. Naturally the preacher is part of the same process. Through the dialogue homily he has to listen and thus become aware of what really is going on in the minds of his young listeners. This enables him to keep his subject at their level: if there is no response to his words then he knows he is not speaking with effect.

Dialogue homilies are not all so easy. Frequently they go off at a tangent away from the main theme; in which case the preacher must make a quick judgement whether to bring the homily back to its central idea, or allow it to continue on its way. This is not to say that dialogue homilies are aimless and uncontrolled. On the contrary: the preacher should know exactly where he is going and how he is getting there. But occasionally he will recognise that a child has hit upon a line of thought which is more fruitful and interesting. In such a case he would be doing a violence to the children's minds if he were roughly to bring them back to the starting point. Yet control is always important. Dialogue does not mean 'free for all'. For those who experience difficulty in controlling children there is no better way to learn than by watching a good teacher at work.

If there has been only one reading (the gospel), a hymn can be sung, or other form of music played, after the homily (D 46). This is not compulsory, but after all the speech, some music, particularly song, might help things along.

4. THE CREED

Many a stout heart sinks at the mere mention of the Creed in connection with Masses for children. And no wonder. It is a densely-packed collection of dogmatic truths promulgated by the Fathers of a General Council in the early years of the Church. It is highly technical, and though relatively short, covers a multitude of theologies. But to balance the disadvantages we must admit that there is a lot to be said for a formula containing the basic truths of our faith; and there is a lot to be said for the proclamation of that faith immediately after the readings and the homily. We should remember also that the Creed is not obligatory at every Mass; that in fact it does not often appear on weekdays.

But it does occur sometimes: and what should we do when celebrating a children's Mass on Sunday? One possibility is the use of the Apostles' Creed, which is more common in schools, instead of the usual Nicene Creed. The only difficulty with that solution lies in the fact that an increasing number of schools is going over to the teaching of the Nicene Creed because of its more frequent use in public (cf D 39 and 49).

Perhaps music is the key to the problem. Adaptation of the text for musical purposes is allowed by the Directory (D 31). However that gives rise to the further problem of how far the adaptation should go. Until now most musicians have regarded this concession as applying to minor alterations in the text. But D 31 speaks of adaptations without specifying any limit other than approval by the 'competent authority' (i.e. the hierarchy). It may well be time therefore for the composition of more radically adapted texts for singing by children. In particular it seems to us that a metrical version of the Creed would be a boon to young Catholics. A simplified Creed might contain separate verses on the following subjects, thus covering the same ground as the historic Creeds: Trinity, Creation, Incarnation, Church, Coming of the Kingdom.

Proposals from other parts of the world have concentrated mainly upon the recited Creed. Here are two examples from manuscript sources: the first is from New Zealand.

I believe in you, O God.
I believe in God the Father who is making all things.
I believe in Jesus whose mother was Mary.
I believe in the Spirit of Jesus who helps us to love.

Amen.

This example has the advantage of being direct and simple. But perhaps it is too simple: its language is not of the best and it omits more than it includes. It is surely important to any Creed that it contain some reference to the Church and to its fulfilment at the end of time.

A better example comes from the United States.

'Dear God, I believe that you made the whole world.
I believe that Jesus is God and man, and died on the cross
   for me.
I believe the Holy Spirit is the third person of the Trinity.
I believe everything the Catholic Church teaches.
Dear Jesus, help me to love you always.'

Perhaps this would be closer to the mark if the final line were to read: 'Dear Jesus, help me to love you so that everybody will know you and be happy with you in your kingdom.'

There is much room here for original ideas. The question we should ask ourselves is: 'Is it necessary to express our faith always in the technical language of Councils? Can the bishops approve more popular, but orthodox expressions of the faith for liturgical use?' A favourable answer to these questions would not mean the total abandonment of the traditional Creeds. They would continue to be taught in the schools, and used at adult Masses.

5. PRAYER OF THE FAITHFUL

God speaks to us in the proclamation of scripture: his voice

143

demands our response. And that is precisely what the Prayer of the Faithful is. It is the response-in-prayer of *these* children to *this* particular reading from the bible.

The ideal is that the response should be immediate and spontaneous because it should be a response, not only to the scripture, but also to the application of the scriptural passage by the homily. But even adults find it hard to respond in a spontaneous manner. Far better that the children compose the prayers ahead of time as part of their general preparation for the celebration. Maybe the teacher or some other adult could be responsible for a spontaneous petition.

The structure of the Prayers of the Faithful varies according to choice. The classic structure is the one used at the Liturgy of Good Friday - announcement of the intention, a pause for silent prayer and summary of everybody's prayer in the 'Collect'. (Indeed this is probably the origin of the present Opening Prayer of the Mass.)

A direct prayer is as valid - 'O God, we ask you to . . .' Maybe not for the purist, but pure liturgy does not often exist outside the text book. Experience shows that this is the form most favoured by the children themselves. In time a little gentle persuading should enable children to write a more traditional form of Prayer and thus influence the future practice of the Sunday Mass.

Most Prayers of the Faithful are prayers of petition (they are sometimes entitled 'Prayer of Intercession'). That is natural because we do depend upon God for everything. But variety is a good thing and thanksgiving is as important a form of prayer as intercession. However, moderation is essential because the Eucharistic Prayer is the major prayer of praise and thanksgiving.

Naturally the children should read their own prayers (D 22). This is most effectively done when each prayer is read by a

different child, either from the front of the class or from his place.

Visual aids work well here (D 36). A class can be divided into preparation groups, each group being responsible not only for a prayer but also for a painting, or cut-out, or collage to illustrate it; this is then held up, or pointed to, during the reading of the prayer. Slides and film can also be useful here.

This is the moment to remind ourselves that after the homily may be a good place for the Penitential Rite, if the Mass has a distinctive penitential theme. A good example of this in practice is the Mass of Ashes on Ash Wednesday where the Penitential Rite, in the form of the blessing and distribution of ashes, comes after the homily.

Chapter 9

GIVE THANKS:
the Offertory and Eucharistic Prayer

Eucharist means to Give Thanks. It is a Greek word which has become part of English liturgical language: and not only English but most other European languages as well. So important is that word and the ideas behind it that it has also become one of the names of the entire Mass. In some parts of the world it is just about the only name. Strictly speaking, eucharist refers to the central part of the Mass which we call the Eucharistic Prayer, or Canon. But if you hear a priest saying he is about to 'celebrate the eucharist' you can be sure he is not going to leave out the Liturgy of the Word and communion but is going to celebrate the entire Mass, from beginning to end.

That is a measure of the importance of eucharist, of Giving Thanks. It really all started with the Jews who were continually thanking God for all that he had done for them. Indeed the two ideas of remembering past mercies and thanking God now are very closely related. That is why our Eucharistic Prayers contain lists (a long one in the fourth Prayer) of the things that God has done, culminating in the passion, death, resurrection and ascension of Jesus.

In the Eucharistic Prayers we use the words and phrases 'calling to mind', 'in memory of', 'memorial'. It is difficult to find words adequate to express the true idea. A 'Memorial' is usually something to help us remember something else - like the Cenotaph in Whitehall which reminds us of those who died in two world wars. But in the bible and liturgy 'memorial', or to 'do in memory', means in some way to make present the thing remembered. That was why Jesus said, 'Do this in memory of me.' Every time we 'do it in memory' of him, he becomes present under the species of bread and wine. And the sacrifice of Calvary ('a single sacrifice for sins', Hebrews 10:12) is made sacramentally present.

All this culminates in one marvellous fact. We give thanks to the Father, not with our own puny words and ideas, but with, in, and through the continued offering of Jesus himself. Jesus is our infallible representative with the Father, our 'hot line to heaven'! And that is why the notion of Giving Thanks Eucharist is so very important (cf D 52).

I. THE OFFERTORY

The official title for this part of the Mass is Preparation of the Gifts. It is a good title because it uses the word 'gifts'. A gift is something freely given in love, or in honour, or in thanksgiving, or in all three, to someone or something else. That is precisely what happens here. The People of God bring their offerings to the altar out of love and thanksgiving to God. More than that. They bring these offerings to show that all they have comes from God in the first place. We have nothing that was not first the gift of God to us.

All sorts of things can be brought to the altar as gifts for God, but the basic gifts are always bread and wine. They are the signs of the basic care and well-being which God continually showers upon us. As gifts they are not much in themselves. Rather, it is what they represent which is so important - God's goodness to us. They also represent our own self-giving to our Father.

The Offertory is a time of much hustle and bustle. The

focus of attention moves from the book to the altar, from listening to doing. Having heard God's voice in scripture, it is now time to reply in thanksgiving, through his Son. It is an exciting time for children. Even at adult Masses the Offertory marks a distinct change in the atmosphere: there is an air of anticipation. It is a time for involvement; there are plenty of things to do and to prepare. What these things are we will discuss in a moment.

But first a word of warning. The official title is *Preparation of the Gifts*. Exciting as this part of the Mass is we should not forget that it is only preparatory. It is not the most important action of the Mass. It is the Eucharistic Prayer which transforms these gifts and makes them acceptable to the Father. The offering of ourselves, which these gifts represent, is made through Christ in the eucharist. Therefore, we should resist the temptation to make too much of the Offertory. Occasionally children's Masses are celebrated in which the Eucharistic Prayer appears to be an apologetic afterthought.

HOW CAN CHILDREN CELEBRATE THE OFFERTORY?

1. *Preparing the altar*
There are two occasions in the Mass when the altar may be prepared, at the very beginning (cf Chapter 7) and here, at the Offertory. There are good arguments for both occasions, but the Offertory is without a doubt the more correct if the children are to do it liturgically. Apart from correctness, preparing the altar at the Offertory provides a dramatic change. Up to now the children have been concentrating largely upon the spoken word, a book (the Bible) and the priest.

Now a sudden change. Attention is turned to a bare table, probably the teacher's desk. Solemnly but swiftly a long white cloth is laid upon it, lighted candles are placed in position. Up to now the altar has been unnecessary. In fact, the Liturgy of the Word could have taken place, if necessary, in another room altogether. But the eucharist demands the use of an altar and therefore it is made ready (cf D 29).

2. *The gifts*

The altar is ready: all that is required is the gifts to be placed on it. The most obvious gifts are the bread and wine, but there are other possibilities. At an adult Mass the Offertory collection is the offering of something of the people themselves, something that they have worked hard for, part of their day to day existence. Precisely the same kind of offering can be made by children. What kind of things are part of the day to day existence of children, what things, if offered at Mass, would symbolise an offering of themselves? Sweets, food, toys, work done in class.

Simple, perhaps, but these are the things that matter in the life of the child. They are of great importance in his necessarily restricted world. Parting with a favourite toy may be as difficult for him as for his father parting with a hard-earned pound note in the Sunday collection plate. Yet it is not the difficulty of offering that counts; what counts is the importance of the offering in the child's scale of values.

There is no doubt that a well-executed item of class work is important to the average child - picture, exercise, handicraft etc. They have even greater importance in the context of a school or classroom Mass because, offered at Mass, they illustrate the fact that the Mass is part of life, that the world can be drawn up into the Mass and that Christ is concerned about everything.

Christmas is a time for offering toys: after the Mass they can be sent to an orphanage for less lucky children. A basket of groceries collected by the children and offered at Mass would make a fine present for the local old folks' home, particularly if the children themselves take it to the home afterwards. However it is not so easy for young children to understand how certain things can be offered to God through the Mass and yet not 'disappear'. This is the case especially with classroom work: there is nobody to take it to - no orphanage that badly needs paintings executed by a class of seven year olds. Will the children feel cheated that their offering has not been 'accepted'? Not necessarily. The astute teacher will see here an opportunity to teach the children that things offered and dedicated to God can quite easily remain part of our daily lives; that in fact the offering was but a symbol of a total self-offering - and yet we will still go on living.

3. *The procession*
The Offertory procession is a sign that the Mass is offered by the people as well as by the priest - 'my sacrifice and yours', says the priest later. The priest is necessary for the valid offering of the Mass, but by placing their gifts upon the altar the laity express the truth that they are co-offerers. So the procession is important (D 34).

Ideally, every child should process to the altar, bringing an offering. If the offering is an altar bread, the child can take it from a nearby box and place it on the paten, at the same time saying 'John' or 'Mary', or whatever the name may be. This is a simple way of showing that each offerer is an individual, not just part of a crowd. If the offerings are things other than the bread and the wine they should be accepted by the priest (with a smile) and placed on a table alongside, or in front of, the altar. Placing them on the altar itself makes it too crowded and untidy: more important, the altar is the table of the sacred meal and we should make every effort not to befuddle that notion by using the altar for 'non-meal' objects.

Space does not always allow a large procession and sometimes we have to compromise by having a procession of a few children representing the others. Alternatively the priest can himself go to each child with the box of altar breads and help them to place an altar bread on the paten which he is also holding. Meanwhile, no matter what method is used, the Offertory is a fine time for a song. It is a sign of unity in offering.

4. *The offertory prayers*
It is just as important that children should see gestures as perform them. Consequently the priest's gestures of offering, first with the bread and then with the wine, should be performed with care and conviction (cf D 33). It is best to wait until the Offertory song has finished: in that way all attention will be upon the celebrant.

The accompanying prayers of offering ('Blessed are you, Lord, God . . .') do not have to be said aloud. Some prefer them in silence because of what they regard as unnecessary repetition of almost identical formula. Yet others sometimes adopt the (unofficial) practice of offering bread and wine together, using a single formula rather as follows:

'Blessed are you, Lord, God of all creation. Through your goodness we have this bread and wine to offer, fruit of the earth and vine, and work of human hands. They will become our spiritual food and drink.'

It has its merits but may not be very helpful for children. They like to see action, the separate and distinct raising up, first of bread then of wine. Much the same thing may be said of the washing of the fingers. Children are used to being made to wash their hands before a meal: what more natural action than that the priest should wash before the eucharistic meal? He may need it, too. After handling gifts, perhaps shaking hands with thirty children, he will need a wash. Nor should the symbolic value of the washing be lost. An occasional explanation of the action, perhaps comparing it with baptism, will impress itself upon the children. That is, if the washing looks like a washing. Priests sometimes have the idea that if an action is a symbol it can be cut down to a minimum. This attitude is wrong. The symbol lies in entire action, properly performed. We should not require people to make an act of faith in the symbol as well as in the thing symbolised. One tiny drop of water on the tips of the fingers is not a symbol of inner purity because it is not an adequate sign of washing. A stream of water over the hands is a different story.

After the action of offering the priest invites the children to pray. This invitation can be made in words of his own choosing (D 23), linking the offering with the theme of the Mass. This is how it might be done:

'Let us pray, children, that God the Father will be pleased with this offering of bread and wine and the basket of food you have collected for the old people.'

or:

'Boys and girls, we are now going to pray that God will accept this offering of bread and wine which is soon to become the body and blood of his Son. We are also going to pray that he will accept this offering of your paintings and class-exercises as a big "thank you" to him for having given us such a lovely term.'

Invitations like these provide a good entry into the Prayer over the Offerings. Ideally the two should be linked together by a common theme. Having first chosen the Prayer, the celebrant can then compose his own invitation. (Regarding the choice of the Prayer over the Offerings, see what we have already discussed in the section on the Opening Prayer in Chapter 7.)

II. THE EUCHARISTIC PRAYER

Over the past eight or ten years the cry has often been heard, 'When are they going to produce a Eucharistic Prayer for children?' Some, impatient of 'they', have used their own privately-composed Prayers. These have varied in quality from superb to sacrilegious. In 1973 the Congregation for Divine Worship sent a letter to the Presidents of all National Conferences of Bishops in which was made an appeal for unity. The Eucharistic Prayer is source and sign of the unity of all in the Church. Its text should therefore be one carrying the approval of all the Church, expressed in approval by central authority.

The 1973 circular letter (referred to henceforth as Letter EP) re-emphasised what can be done within the present structure of the Mass by way of variations, and made a few more suggestions of its own as to what could be done with the present four official Eucharistic Prayers. But new Prayers were not ruled out altogether. We will first take a look at the possibilities available in the official Eucharistic Prayers; then we shall look to the future and the advent of completely new texts.

1. *Adapting the four official Eucharistic Prayers*
A word of introduction often transforms a familiar text. We have already emphasised this point when speaking of things like the readings: it applies equally to the Eucharistic Prayer (cf Letter EP 8). The introduction at this part of the Mass reminds the congregation why, for what motive, the

great thanksgiving is being made. 'Children, in the big prayer I am going to say now, we will thank God for all the wonderful things he has done for us. But especially we are going to thank him for all the good things he has done for us in school this term.' With a little prompting the children can also express their own thanksgiving motives - 'I want to thank God for . . .'

Then comes the Preface, remembering that its opening dialogue should not be adapted (cf D 39 and Chapter 7 above). The Preface is part of the Eucharistic Prayer and is one of the most variable parts of the Mass. The new Roman Missal contains 84 Prefaces (82 plus 2 from the Second and Fourth Eucharistic Prayers), which makes virtually certain that every aspect of salvation is covered. Naturally, at major feasts and seasons we should abide by the appropriate Preface; but at other times there is no need always to follow the 'Common' daily Preface. Instead, a spirit of flexibility will do a power of good by setting the Eucharistic Prayer off along a particular theme (cf Letter EP 8). Note that this document is primarily concerned with adult Masses. (How often does the celebrant repeat the same old Preface? How many celebrants know about the rich variety of Prefaces? How many have copies of the texts?) To make selection easier, the Index of the Roman Missal lists all the Prefaces separately along with a summary of the theme; for example, Sunday Preface V has for theme 'Man's place in creation.'

That leaves us with the texts of four Eucharistic Prayers. Is that the limit of choice and adaptation? No. Although intercessions belong more properly to the Prayers of the Faithful, yet they do find a place in the eucharistic part of the liturgy and, notably in the First Prayer, a place is provided for particular intentions of the living and the dead (cf Letter EP 9). Admittedly not much of an adaptation, but it is something. In addition certain seasons of the year (e.g. Christmas,

Easter and Pentecost) are marked by special variations in the prayer texts of the First Prayer; and Ritual Masses (e.g. ordination) also have special variations (cf Letter EP 10).

What has all that got to do with children's Masses? Simply this. A brief paragraph at the end of Letter EP 10 says there is no reason why episcopal conferences, or individual bishops for their own dioceses, should not compose more variations like those mentioned above and submit them for Rome's approval. The possibilities suddenly multiply. Variations, specially written for children's Masses and designed to fit into our present four Eucharistic Prayers, could be written and receive, through the bishop, official approval. (Going through an episcopal conference is necessarily a longer process.) Perhaps some diocesan liturgical commission would take such a project upon itself. Liturgical creativity at a local level would certainly be welcome.

There is yet another interesting suggestion contained in Letter EP 10 which deserves separate consideration. At present we are accustomed to three acclamations in the Eucharistic Prayer - the Sanctus, after the consecration, and the concluding 'Amen'. Why not more? The Letter appears to suggest this and some experts have acted upon it. The idea is to divide a Eucharistic Prayer into its various 'sense sections' so that, at a natural break in the recitation, the congregation can lift up its collective voice in an acclamation. An example from the Fourth Prayer will illustrate the idea:

Priest: 'Father, we acknowledge your greatness:
all your actions show your wisdom and love.
You formed man in your likeness
and set him over the whole world
to serve you, his creator,
and to rule over all creatures.

People: Father, it is right that we should give you thanks
and glory.

Priest: Even when he disobeyed you and lost your friendship
you did not abandon him to the power of death,
but helped all men to seek and find you.

People: Father, it is right that we should give you thanks
and glory.'

The possibilities of this sort of thing at a children's Mass
should be clear enough. Frequent acclamations not only
make a better understanding of what the Prayer means and
that it is their Prayer as well as the priest's. Variable acclamations will avoid the danger of a merely mechanical response.

There is no doubt that the best answer lies in Eucharistic
Prayers specially composed for children. Until the official
texts are translated and even afterwards, there are many
possibilities for the adaptation of the present four Prayers. In
addition, celebrants can do much by the way they recite the
Eucharistic Prayer (D 52). Even the most difficult of texts
can be made intelligible by good reading - and the simplest
can be destroyed by lack of care and understanding.

At this point it is well to remind ourselves that brevity
does not always mean clarity. There is a growing body of
opinion that Eucharistic Prayer IV is more intelligible to
children than is II. The latter packs more theology into a
smaller space: the former spreads it out into more easily
assimilated concepts.

2. *New Eucharistic Prayers*
You don't have to look far to find Eucharistic Prayers for
children. Dozens of them have been in circulation for some
years. In the British Isles they have no official standing -
which is just as well because most of them are theologically

unsound and owe little to the eucharistic tradition of the Church.

Yet that is not to say that they should never have been written. How else are we to arrive at suitable texts if we do not first explore all the possibilities? Finding new texts for the liturgy has always been largely a matter of selection from pre-existing material rather than fresh composition. The proliferation of texts is also an indication of a need. And there is a need for children's Eucharistic Prayers, let there be no mistake about it. In this Prayer we are dealing not only with the central and most solemn part of the Mass but also with the central act of the community, the Church. We must identify ourselves with the action and words of the Prayer - it is ours. Do children feel that? Is their 'Amen' a true assent to what has been said in their name?

They must certainly know that something very special is happening, that bread and wine are being changed into the body and blood of Christ. But there is so much more to it than that which can be obscured by language which is too adult. Once again we are back at the truth that *this* Mass is the worship of *these* children. The words and gestures should contribute to making that a reality.

After all, there is nothing exclusive about the texts of the four adult Eucharistic Prayers. For centuries the Church used an amazingly wide variety of texts. In parts of Spain the Eucharistic Prayer changed as often as the Collect - principally because the entire Mass text was linked by a common theme. Today Eastern Catholics use quite different versions from those in the West.

Even official children's Eucharistic Prayers have existed for some time. The Congregation for Divine Worship approved a Eucharistic Prayer for use at first communion Masses in the Philippines (though the Prayer was not very distinguished). In 1973, an approved children's Prayer was used at the Melbourne Eucharistic Congress. Apart from these, dozens of other Eucharistic Prayers have been approved for local use by individual bishops and hierarchies.

Finally, in 1974, Rome published the texts of three Eucharistic Prayers for young children. As far as one can tell, they will be the answer to a great need. However, much depends upon suitable translations. Fortunately, the document containing the new Prayers emphasises the need for a translation which reflects local needs; in other words, the Prayers are open to a certain amount of adaptation. Rome appears to be more concerned with the underlying structure of the Prayers than with the actual words.

These new Prayers, when they come, may be just what we have been looking for. Or they may not. What appears fine in one language, may not be suitable in translation. Fortunately the matter need not end there. Letter EP 6 actually welcomes the submission to the Congregation of Divine Worship of new Eucharistic Prayers for approval. Anglo-Saxon Catholic attitudes have tended to regard communications with Rome as a one-way affair: Rome decrees and we obey. That is fine up to a point but communications must also go in the opposite direction, and that is exactly what Rome is asking us to do. Instead of merely accepting the texts handed down from Roman curial offices we should also be submitting for approval Eucharistic Prayers of our own which are not translations but have grown from a real, local need.

Some priests and teachers will not take kindly to the insistence upon official approval. It is necessary. A large number of the unofficial texts circulating in Britain do not express the faith of the Church. The Eucharistic Prayer is a prayer of unity - unity with the local community, unity with the universal Church. If the faith expressed in a prayer is not that of the Church then it is no longer a prayer of unity but rather of disunity (cf Letter EP 11). This is not to rule out controlled experimentation: there is no sense in submitting for approval a Prayer if you do not first know that it will be successful with the people who will use it.

There is a need for the composition of new Eucharistic Prayers. But that is easier said than done. A Eucharistic Prayer is no ordinary prayer; it is governed by a structure which has been with the Church almost from the very beginning. What this structure is can be seen very clearly in the General Instruction on the Roman Missal 55. Using that paragraph as the basis, here is the structure together with a few comments:

a. *Thanksgiving*   The Preface is the best example of this, but often the theme of Thanksgiving spills over into other parts of the Eucharistic Prayer. The Fourth Prayer is a good example of this.

b. *Acclamation*   i.e. 'Holy, Holy, Holy'. This must always be included.

c. *Epiclesis*   A call upon God to make the bread and wine the body and blood of Christ. In the Second, Third and Fourth Prayers the call is directed to the Holy Spirit. It takes place when the priest stretches out his hands over the bread and wine.

d. *Consecration*   This takes place during an account of the institution of the Eucharist at the Last Supper.

e. *Anamnesis - Memorial*   The 'calling to mind' which we discussed earlier in this chapter.

f. *Oblation*   With the words 'we offer you' in the present four official prayers. This is important because it explains what the prayer is all about – the offering of the sacrificial victim in thanksgiving and praise.

g. *Intercessions* The aim here is unity in the body of Christ. 'May all of us . . . be brought together in unity by the Holy Spirit.' In the three new Eucharistic Prayers, this part of the Prayer always refers to the Holy Spirit because he is the principle of unity of the Church. Just as the Holy Spirit was called down to change bread and wine into Christ's body and blood (cf c.), so now we call upon the Spirit to come down upon all men to make them the Mystical Body of Christ.

h. *Doxology* i.e. 'Through him . . .' etc. This marvellous summary of the role of Christ is concluded by the people's 'Amen', an act of assent to the entire Eucharistic Prayer.

This is the briefest summary of the Eucharistic Prayer. Anyone who attempts the composition of a new Prayer, for adults or children, should have completed a far deeper study than that. Books such as Louis Bouyer's *Eucharist*, or *The Shape of the Eucharist* by Gregory Dix provide deeper reading.

Chapter 10

TAKE AND EAT:
Communion

The context of the central part of the Mass is a sacrificial meal. From the Offertory onwards most of the action centres upon food - bread and wine which becomes the body and blood of Christ. Like any food, it is meant to be eaten and drunk.

Not everybody likes the Mass being referred to as a meal. They prefer 'banquet', 'paschal supper', 'sacrificial meal' - which all come down to the same thing in the end. Eating and drinking is a meal, whether you call it a banquet or a supper. A large number of Jesus's disciples left him because he said he was the food of life and that they would have to eat his flesh and drink his blood. He did not call them back by explaining that he was really talking about a sacrificial banquet (cf John 6).

Communion is the time for eating and drinking. Everything in this part of the Mass either leads up to it or is in thanksgiving for it. The danger is that the central act - receiving communion - can be obscured by too many prayers and actions. Simplicity and directness are particularly important for children. Therefore the Directory, in paragraph 53, provides for the utmost simplicity and directness. This paragraph must be interpreted as it stands: it is as important for what it omits as for what it includes.

At communion, all that is necessary are the Lord's Prayer, the Breaking of Bread and the Invitation to Communion. All the other elements - 'Embolism', Prayer of Peace, Sign of Peace, Lamb of God, the priest's preparatory prayers - may be omitted. Which is not to say that they should be omitted at every Mass. Varying circumstances require varying solutions. A Mass for very young children may be the better for the omission of some of the pre-communion elements. On the other hand, older children will need to become accustomed to the adult form of the Mass.

In the discussion that follows we will deal with all the possibilities.

1. *The Lord's Prayer*
This is the central prayer of our faith. First taught to us by Christ himself, it expresses the depths of our relationship with God. It comes at this part of the Mass, not only because of its obvious reference to 'our daily bread', but also because communion is a deepening of our relationship as children of the Father. For these reasons this sacred text may never be altered (D 39). But there is plenty of scope for adaptation in the priest's introduction (D 23).

It is important to take advantage of the facility to adapt here. The introduction to the Lord's Prayer comes after a relatively lengthy Prayer which most likely will not have made any direct reference to the theme of this particular Mass: it also comes before more official, unchangeable texts. A reference at this point to the theme will help the children relate the theme with the Mass. It is the time for a short introduction, not a homily. Good examples of introductions may be found by the priest in the appendix to the new edition of *The Divine Office*. Here are some designed to link the Lord's Prayer with Mass themes:

Mass for old people:
'Our mothers and fathers look after us. Let us pray to God our Father that he will look after the old people who have nobody.'

Mass for a new term:
'There are so many things to learn and do. We are now going to ask God to teach us and look after us because he is our Father and loves us always.'

Mass for peace:
'God is our Father and he wants everybody in the world to be like brothers and sisters. Let's pray to him that people will stop hating and killing each other.'

An interesting way of composing an introduction is by selecting one of the petitions of the Lord's Prayer and making it a motive of prayer. For example:

Hallowed be thy name:
'God wants everybody to love and respect his name. Let us pray to him that we will always keep his name holy.'

Give us this day our daily bread:
'Jesus is our Bread of life in communion. Let us pray to the Father that we will have that bread always.'

Although the text of the Lord's prayer may not be altered, there is much to be said for singing it. Perhaps the new setting in the Missal may come to compare with the old Latin version in uniting whole congregations in song. The Lord's Prayer should be our 'National Anthem'.

2. *Embolism ('Deliver us, Lord' . . .)*
This prayer, immediately following the Lord's Prayer, is not compulsory at children's Masses (cf D 53). An interesting adaptation of the prayer consists of including extra 'evils' from which the community prays to be delivered. For example:

'Deliver us, Lord, from every evil,
from famine,

163

from homelessness,
from war,
and grant us peace in our day . . .'

So far as is known, this form of adaptation has no official approval, but it certainly deserves consideration.

3. The Rite of Peace

Another item which may be omitted (cf D 53). But is not a prayer for peace rather important in these times? The sign of peace is avoided in many children's Masses: is it not among children that community and fellowship are most natural? What then more fitting than for the children to exchange some sign of that fellowship? Occasionally it may be possible for the priest to shake the hand of each child - after greeting the class teacher: adult example is the best of teachers.

An alternative method, often practised with great success, is for the whole community, children and adults, to hold hands around the altar while singing the Lord's Prayer. It is an illustration that we are all sons and daughters of the Father, and brothers and sisters of each other.

4. Lamb of God

Again, this may be omitted (cf D 53). Strictly speaking, it is intended to accompany the action of the Breaking of the Bread, and should the Breaking continue for some time (as, for instance, when one large piece of Bread is being used for all the communicants) the singing can be repeated as long as is required (cf D 31). However, considering the importance of the action of the Breaking, it is often better to leave out the Lamb of God altogether so that the children can watch what is happening.

5. *The Breaking of Bread*

This may never be omitted (D 53). The very title was the earliest known name for the Mass. Down through the ages it has received various interpretations, some scriptural, others merely pious. To the apostles it was the sign of the Lord (Luke 24:30) and a symbol of their unity in the one body of Christ. For this reason, it is helpful if the bread is one large piece so that each communicant can see even more clearly the symbolism of sharing in the one body of Christ. If this cannot be done then half the priest's own host should be broken into two or three pieces for the younger communicants.

It is important that the priest should make the Breaking of the Bread a momentuous ceremony with the host lifted well above the altar and not hidden down behind the chalice.

The priest's preparatory prayers ('Lord Jesus Christ . . .') are private and should never be said aloud (GI 56f; 114).

6. *Invitation to Communion*

This may never be omitted (D 53) but the priest may use his own words (D 23). One method is to insert a phrase within the official text:

'This is the Lamb of God who takes away the sins of the world and who wants us to love one another. Happy are those who are called to his supper.'

Another method is to compose a completely new text:

'This is Jesus who died for us and then rose from the dead. He gives himself to us like this to make us more like him. We will ask him to make us ready to receive him in communion.'

A practical point: some celebrants, having broken the host,

put it together again as if it were still a single piece. What they show to the congregation appears to be an unbroken host. This is not correct. If the Fraction, or Breaking of Bread, is to mean anything then it must be seen to mean something.

7. *Receiving communion*

The Directory twice (D 34 and 54) refers to the devotion and tranquillity needed for receiving the Lord at communion. Easier said than done. Any movement of a group of young children runs the risk of developing into chaos At the same time it would be wrong to control children in the manner of a sergeant major. Obviously a procession helps, but an alternative method is for the priest to come to the children. This is especially helpful when the children are already in a circle around the altar and there is no obstructing furniture.

If the priest knows the children well, or if each child has his or her name pinned prominently, he can say, as he gives communion, 'The body of Christ, Mary' or '. . . John'.

Singing is a problem at this particular moment. The communion hymn is often better sung if left until the priest has completed the communions. Large groups of children are able to sustain the singing: rarely can small groups do so.

After communion a little silent prayer is welcome after all the singing, praying aloud and movement. Sitting quietly and relaxed, the children are in an ideal mood for prayer. What they need is prompting. A child rises and says, 'We are going to thank God for . . .' and names an intention. After twenty or thirty seconds of silent prayer another child rises (at the teacher's signal) and proclaims another intention. The priest or teacher can of course be the prompters. The who or the how is not important: recollection and prayer is the one important thing.

Finally the priest recites the Prayer after Communion. This is a good opportunity for joining into one prayer the theme of the Mass, the fact of Christ's coming in Communion and some form of resolution for the future.

Chapter 11

GO:
The End of the Mass

A short chapter for the shortest part of the Mass. Yet it is just as important as the other parts. The end of the Mass is, as it were, an opening of the Mass out to the whole world. In the words of a celebrant this writer once heard: 'Go in peace. The Mass is not ended.' He had a good point. Christ came to save the whole world, all people, all ages. The Mass is that act of redemption and must have an influence upon the world in which we live. If not, Christ is powerless. The aim of this part of the Mass is to send the children out in the power of God (cf D 15). Whatever relevance the Mass has for them depends to a large extent on the way in which the priest concludes.

Just as the Mass began with a short introduction after the greeting, so now, before the final blessing, it can conclude with a brief word from the priest reminding the children what the Mass was about, what lessons they have learnt from it and what difference it should make to their daily lives (D 54). One method of solemnising this conclusion is by delivering it in the form of a Prayer over the People (e.g. 'Lord, help these children, whom you have strengthened with the body of your Son in communion, to go out and always be on the look-out for old people who need help').

The blessing which follows must conclude with the usual Trinitarian formula - but the Directory lays down no other rules (D 39, 54). Naturally the familiar 'May almighty God bless you . . .' is adequate, but a more solemn form might be more suitable. To the priest a classroom Mass may be a weekly duty, but to the child it is a once-a-term treat. The new Missal contains a fair selection of solemn blessings; however it will be difficult to find one expressing the theme of the Mass and at the level of the children. Once again the solution lies in the do-it-yourself policy. It is not too difficult if one remembers that a solemn blessing has three parts corresponding to the Persons of the Trinity. And remember to keep it short. Here is an example:

Telling people about Jesus:
'May God the Father protect you and guide you when you stand up for his Son.
Amen.
May Jesus be always in your heart so that other people may see him in you.
Amen.
May the Holy Spirit give you courage and help you to say and do the right thing.
Amen.
And may the blessing of . . .'

The dismissal also can be adapted:
'The Mass is ended. Now go out to tell people about Jesus.'
Finally the recessional hymn. In character it is very similar to the entry hymn. The hymn should be appropriate to the Mass theme - that is, if it is a hymn; instrumental music is sometimes a better choice. The priest goes out: with the children, or on his own: after packing his equipment, or leaving that for later. And the children? By now, they will be ready for some play.

Conclusion
Nothing sums up all that this book has tried to do better than the final paragraph of the Directory:

'The contents of the Directory are intended to help children quickly and joyfully to encounter Christ together in the eucharistic celebration and to stand in the presence of the Father with him. If they are formed by conscious and active participation in the eucharistic sacrifice and meal, they should learn day by day, at home and away from home, to proclaim Christ to others among their family and among their peers, by living the "faith, which expresses itself through love" (Galatians 5:6).'

Appendix I

CHECK LIST
The possibilities of adaptation and who may prepare them

Ideally, the priest, lay leader (teacher, catechist or parent) and children should together carry out the preparation. However, in this check list we indicate those who have the prime responsibility for adapting particular items of the Mass:

Entrance Song	Lay leader
Greeting	Priest
Introduction	Priest/lay leader
Penitential Rite: various forms (may occasionally be left until after Gospel)	Priest/lay leader
Lord, have mercy (music)	Lay leader
(Glory be to God on High) (music)	Lay leader
Opening Prayer (with introduction)	Priest (or Priest/lay leader)
Readings and Chants (1) and (2)	Lay leader
3 Gospel (drama)	Lay leader
Homily (dialogue)	Priest/lay leader
(Penitential Rite) see above	Priest/lay leader
Prayers of Faithful	Lay leader (perhaps Priest/ lay leader)
(Offertory Procession)	Lay leader
(Offertory Song)	Lay leader
Invitation to pray	Priest
Prayer over the Offerings	Priest (or Priest/lay leader)

(Introduction to Eucharistic Prayer)	Priest
(Thanksgiving within Preface— special intentions)	Priest/lay leader
Holy, Holy, Holy (music)	Lay leader
Eucharistic Prayer: which one?	Priest/lay leader
(additional acclamations)	Priest/lay leader
Our Father: (special introduction)	Priest
(music)	Lay leader
(Embolism i.e. prayer following Our Father)	Priest
(prayer for peace)	Priest
Invitation to Communion: (special)	Priest
(Communion Song)	Lay leader
Final Prayer	Priest (or Priest/lay leader)
(Final admonition/instruction)	Priest
(Prayer over People)	Priest
(Solemn Blessing)	Priest
Dismissal	Priest
Recessional Song	Lay leader

DIRECTORY FOR MASSES WITH CHILDREN

CONTENTS

Appendix II

INTRODUCTION

1. The Church shows special concern for baptised children who have yet to be fully initiated through the sacraments of confirmation and eucharist as well as for children who have only recently been admitted to holy communion. Today the circumstances in which children grow up are not favourable to their spiritual progress.[1] In addition, sometimes parents barely fulfil the obligations of Christian education which they undertake at the baptism of their children.

2. In bringing up children in the Church a special difficulty arises from the fact that liturgical celebrations, especially the eucharist, cannot fully exercise their innate pedagogical force upon children.[2] Although the mother tongue may now be used at Mass, still the words and signs have not been sufficiently adapted to the capacity of children.

In fact, even in daily life children cannot always understand everything that they experience with adults, and they easily become weary. It cannot be expected, moreover, that everything in the liturgy will always be intelligible to them. Nonetheless, we may fear spiritual harm if over the years children repeatedly experience in the Church things that are scarcely comprehensible to them: recent psychological study has established how profoundly children are formed by the religious experience of infancy and early childhood, according to their individual religious capacity.[3]

3. The Church follows its Master, who 'put his arms around the children . . . and blessed them' (Mark 10:16). It cannot leave chil-

dren to themselves. The Second Vatican Council had spoken in the Constitution on the Liturgy about the need of liturgical adaptation for various groups.[4] Soon afterwards, especially in the first Synod of Bishops held in Rome in 1967, the Church began to consider how participation of children could be made easier. On the occasion of the Synod the president of the Consilium for the Implementation of the Constitution on the Liturgy said explicitly that it could not be a matter of 'creating some entirely special rite but rather of retaining, shortening, or omitting some elements or of making a better selection of texts'.[5]

4. All the details of eucharistic celebration with a congregation were determined in the General Instruction of the revised *Roman Missal*, published in 1969. Then this congregation began to prepare a special directory for Masses with children, as a supplement to the instruction. This was done in response to repeated petitions from the entire Catholic world and with the cooperation of men and women specialists from almost every nation.

5. Like the General Instruction, this directory reserves some adaptations to conferences of bishops or individual bishops.[6]
With regard to adaptations of the Mass which may be necessary for children in a given country but which cannot be included in this general directory, the conferences of bishops should submit proposals to the Apostolic See, in accord with article 40 of the Constitution on the Liturgy. These adaptations are to be introduced only with the consent of the Apostolic See.

6. The directory is concerned with children who have not yet entered the period of pre-adolescence. It does not speak directly of children who are physically or mentally retarded because a broader adaptation is sometimes necessary for them.[7] Nevertheless, the following norms may also be applied to the retarded, with the necessary changes.

7. The first chapter of the directory (nos. 8-15) gives a kind of foundation by considering the different ways in which children

are introduced to the eucharistic liturgy. The second chapter briefly treats Masses with adults, in which children also take part (nos. 16-19). Finally, the third chapter (nos. 20-54) treats at greater length Masses with children, in which only some adults take part.

CHAPTER I

The Introduction of Children to the Eucharistic Celebration

8. A fully Christian life cannot be conceived without participation in the liturgical services in which the faithful, gathered into a single assembly, celebrate the paschal mystery. Therefore, the religious initiation of children must be in harmony with this purpose.[8] By baptising infants, the Church expresses its confidence in the gifts received from this sacrament; thus it must be concerned that the baptised grow in communion with Christ and the brethren. Sharing in the eucharist is the sign and pledge of this very communion. Children are prepared for eucharistic communion and introduced more deeply into its meaning. It is not right to separate such liturgical and eucharistic formation from the general human and Christian education of children. Indeed it would be harmful if liturgical formation lacked such a foundation.

9. For this reason all who have a part in the formation of children should consult and work together. In this way even if children already have some feeling for God and the things of God, they may also experience the human values which are found in the eucharistic celebration, depending upon their age and personal progress. These values are the activity of the community, exchange of greetings, capacity to listen and to seek and grant pardon, expression of gratitude, experience of symbolic actions, a meal of friendship, and festive celebration.[9]

Eucharistic catechesis, which is mentioned in no. 12, should go beyond such human values. Thus, depending on their age, psychological condition, and social situation, children may gradually open their minds to the perception of Christian values and the celebration of the mystery of Christ. [10]

10.   The Christian family has the greatest role in teaching these Christian and human values.[11] Thus Christian education, provided by parents and other educators, should be strongly encouraged in relation to liturgical formation of children as well.

By reason of the responsibility freely accepted at the baptism of their children, parents are bound in conscience to teach them gradually to pray. This they do by praying with them each day and by introducing them to prayers said privately.[12] If children are prepared in this way, even from their early years, and do take part in the Mass with their family when they wish, they will easily begin to sing and to pray in the liturgical community, indeed they will have some kind of foretaste of the eucharistic mystery.

If the parents are weak in faith but still wish their children to receive Christian formation, at least they should be urged to share the human values mentioned above with their children. On occasion, they should be encouraged to participate in meetings of parents and in non-eucharistic celebrations with their children.

11.   The Christian communities to which the individual families belong or in which the children live also have a responsibility toward children baptised in the Church. By giving witness to the Gospel, living fraternal charity, actively celebrating the mysteries of Christ, the Christian community is the best school of Christian and liturgical formation for the children who live in it.

Within the Christian community, godparents and others with special concern who are moved by apostolic zeal can help greatly in the necessary catechesis of children of families which are unable to fulfil their own responsibility in Christian education.

In particular these ends can be served by preschool programmes, Catholic schools, and various kinds of classes for children.

12.   Even in the case of children, the liturgy itself always exerts its own proper didactic force.[13] Yet within programmes of

catechetical, scholastic, and parochial formation, the necessary importance should be given to catechesis on the Mass.[14] This catechesis should be directed to the child's active, conscious, and authentic participation.[15] 'Clearly accommodated to the age and mentality of the children, it should attempt, through the principal rites and prayers, to convey the meaning of the Mass, including a participation in the whole life of the Church.'[16] This is especially true of the text of the eucharistic prayer and of the acclamations with which the children take part in this prayer.

Special mention should be made of the catechesis through which children are prepared for first communion. Not only should they learn the truths of faith concerning the eucharist, but they should also understand how from first communion on – prepared by penance according to their need and fully initiated into the body of Christ – they may actively participate in the eucharist with the people of God and have their place at the Lord's table and in the community of the brethren.

13.   Various kinds of celebrations may also play a major role in the liturgical formation of children and in their preparation for the Church's liturgical life. By the very fact of celebration children easily come to appreciate some liturgical elements, for example, greetings, silence, and common praise (especially when this is sung in common). Such celebrations, however, should avoid having too didactic a character.

14.   Depending on the capacity of the children, the word of God should have a greater and greater place in these celebrations. In fact, as the spiritual capacity of children develops, celebrations of the word of God in the strict sense should be held frequently, especially during Advent and Lent.[17] These will help greatly to develop in the children an appreciation of the word of God.

15.   Over and above what has been said already, all liturgical and eucharistic formation should be directed toward a greater and greater response to the gospel in the daily life of the children.

CHAPTER II

Masses with Adults in Which Children Also Participate

16. Parish Masses are celebrated in many places, especially on Sundays and Holy days, with a large number of adults and a smaller number of children. On such occasions the witness of adult believers can have a great effect upon the children. Adults can also benefit spiritually from experiencing the part which the children have within the Christian community. If children take part in these Masses together with their parents and other members of their family, this should be of great help to the Christian spirit of families.

Infants who as yet are unable or unwilling to take part in the Mass may be brought in at the end of Mass to be blessed together with the rest of the community. This may be done, for example, if parish helpers have been taking care of them in a separate area.

17. Nevertheless, in Masses of this kind it is necessary to take great care that the children do not feel neglected because of their inability to participate or to understand what happens and what is proclaimed in the celebration. Some account should be taken of their presence, for example, by speaking to them directly in the introductory comments (as at the beginning and the end of Mass) and in part of the homily.

Sometimes, moreover, it will perhaps be appropriate, if the physical arrangements and the circumstances of the community permit, to celebrate the liturgy of the word, including a homily, with the children in a separate area that is not too far removed. Then, before the eucharistic liturgy begins, the children are led to the place where the adults have meanwhile been celebrating their own liturgy of the word.

18. It may also be very helpful to give some tasks to the children. They may, for example, bring forward the gifts or sing one or other of the parts of Mass.

19.   Sometimes, if the number of children is large, it may be suitable to plan the Masses so that they correspond better to the needs of the children. In this case the homily should be directed to the children but in such a way that adults may also benefit from it. In addition to the adaptations now in the Order of Mass, one or other of the special adaptations described below may be employed in a Mass celebrated with adults in which children also participate, where the bishop permits such adaptations.

CHAPTER III

Masses with Children in Which Only a Few Adults Participate

20.   In addition to the Masses in which children take part with their parents and other members of their family (which are not always possible everywhere), Masses with children in which only some adults take part are recommended, especially during the week. From the beginning of the liturgical restoration it has been clear to everyone that some adaptations are necessary in these Masses.[18]

Such adaptations, but only those of a more general kind, will be considered below (nos. 38-54).

21.   It is always necessary to keep in mind that through these eucharistic celebrations children must be led towards the celebration of Mass with adults, especially the Masses in which the Christian community comes together on Sundays.[19] Thus, apart from adaptations which are necessary because of the children's age, the result should not be entirely special rites which differ too greatly from the Order of Mass celebrated with a congregation.[20] The purpose of the various elements should always correspond with what is said in the General Instruction of the *Roman Missal* on individual points, even if at times for pastoral reasons an absolute *identity* cannot be insisted upon.

OFFICES AND MINISTRIES IN THE CELEBRATION

22.   The principles of active and conscious participation are in a sense even more valid for Masses celebrated with children. Every effort should be made to increase this participation and to make it more intense. For this reason as many children as possible should have special parts in the celebration, for example: preparing the place and the altar (see no. 29), acting as cantor (see no. 24), singing in a choir, playing musical instruments (see no. 32), proclaiming the readings (see nos. 24 and 47), responding during the homily (see no. 48), reciting the intentions of the general intercessions, bringing the gifts to the altar, and performing similar activities to accord with the usage of various communities (see no. 34).

To encourage participation it will sometimes be helpful to have several additions, for example, the insertion of motives for giving thanks before the priest begins the dialogue of the preface.

In all this one should keep in mind that external activities will be fruitless and even harmful if they do not serve the internal participation of the children. Thus religious silence has its importance even in Masses with children (see no. 37). The children should not be allowed to forget that all the forms of participation reach their high point in eucharistic communion when the body and blood of Christ are received as spiritual nourishment.[21]

23.   It is the responsibility of the priest who celebrates with children to make the celebration festive, fraternal, meditative.[22] Even more than in Masses with adults, the priest should try to bring about this kind of spirit. It will depend upon his personal preparation and his manner of acting and speaking with others.

Above all, the priest should be concerned about the dignity, clarity, and simplicity of his actions and gestures. In speaking to the children he should express himself so that he will be easily understood, while avoiding any childish style of speech.

The free use of introductory comments[23] will lead children to a genuine liturgical participation, but these explanations should not be merely didactic.

It will help in reaching the hearts of the children if the priest sometimes uses his own words when he gives invitations, for example, at the penitential rite, the prayer over the gifts, the Lord's Prayer, the sign of peace, and communion.

24.   Since the eucharist is always the action of the entire Church community, the participation of at least some adults is desirable. These should be present not as monitors but as participants, praying with the children and helping them to the extent necessary.

With the consent of the pastor or the rector of the church, one of the adults may speak to the children after the gospel, especially if the priest finds it difficult to adapt himself to the mentality of the children. In this matter the norms of the Congregation for the Clergy should be observed.

The diversity of ministries should also be encouraged in Masses with children so that the Mass may be evidently the celebration of a community.[24] For example, readers and cantors, whether children or adults, should be employed. In this way variety will keep the children from becoming tired because of the sameness of voices.

PLACE AND TIME OF CELEBRATION

25.   The primary place for the eucharistic celebration for children is the church. Within the church, however, a space should be carefully chosen, if available, which will be suited to the number of participants. It should be a place where the children can conduct themselves freely according to the demands of a living liturgy that is suited to their age.

If the church does not satisfy these demands, it will sometimes be suitable to celebrate the eucharist with children outside a sacred place. Then the place chosen should be appropriate and worthy.[25]

26.   The time of day chosen for Masses with children should correspond with the circumstances of their lives so that they may

be most open to hearing the word of God and to celebrating the eucharist.

27. Weekday Mass in which children participate can certainly be celebrated with greater effect and less danger of weariness if it does not take place every day (for example, in boarding schools). Moreover, preparation can be more careful if there is a longer interval between celebrations.

Sometimes it is preferable to have common prayer to which the children may contribute spontaneously, either a common meditation or a celebration of the word of God. These celebrations continue the eucharist and lead to deeper participation in later eucharistic celebrations.

28. When the number of children who celebrate the eucharist together is very great, attentive and conscious participation becomes more difficult. Therefore, if possible, several groups should be formed; these should not be set up rigidly according to age but with regard to the progress of religious formation and catechetical preparation of the children.

During the week such groups may be invited to the sacrifice of the Mass on different days.

PREPARATION FOR THE CELEBRATION

29. Each eucharistic celebration with children should be carefully prepared beforehand, especially with regard to prayers, songs, readings, and intentions of the general intercessions. This should be done in discussion with the adults and with the children who will have a special ministry in these Masses. If possible, some of the children should take part in preparing and ornamenting the place of celebration and preparing the chalice with the paten and cruets. Over and above the appropriate internal participation, such activity will help to develop the spirit of community celebration.

SINGING AND MUSIC

30.   Singing is of great importance in all celebrations, but it is to be especially encouraged in every way for Masses celebrated with children, in view of their special affinity for music.[26]. The culture of various groups and the capabilities of the children present should be taken into account.

If possible the acclamations should be sung by the children rather than recited, especially the acclamations which are a part of the eucharistic prayer.

31.   To facilitate the children's participation in singing the Gloria, profession of faith, Sanctus, and Agnus Dei, it is permissible to use music set to appropriate vernacular texts, accepted by the competent authority, even if these do not agree completely with the liturgical texts.[27]

32.   The use of 'musical instruments may be of great help' in Masses with children, especially if they are played by the children themselves.[28] The playing of instruments will help to support the singing or to encourage the reflection of the children: sometimes by themselves instruments express festive joy and the praise of God.

Care should always be taken, however, that the music does not prevail over the singing or become a distraction rather than a help to the children. Music should correspond to the purpose which is attached to the different periods for which it is introduced into the Mass.

With these precautions and with special and necessary concern, music that is technically produced may be also used in Masses with children, in accord with norms established by the conferences of bishops.

GESTURES AND ACTIONS

33.   The development of gestures, postures, and actions is very important for Masses with children in view of the nature of the

liturgy as an activity of the entire man and in view of the psychology of children. This should be done in harmony with the age and local usage. Much depends not only on the actions of the priest,[29] but also on the manner in which the children conduct themselves as a community.

If a conference of bishops, in accord with the norm of the General Instruction of the *Roman Missal*[30] adapts the actions of the Mass to the mentality of the people, it should give consideration to the special condition of children or should determine such adaptations for children only.

34. Among the actions which are considered under this heading, processions deserve special mention as do other activities which involve physical participation.

The processional entrance of the children with the priest may help them to experience a sense of the communion that is thus constituted.[31] The participation of at least some children in the procession with the book of gospels makes clear the presence of Christ who announces His word to the people. The procession of children with the chalice and the gifts expresses clearly the value and meaning of the preparation of gifts. The communion procession, if properly arranged, helps greatly to develop the piety of the children.

VISUAL ELEMENTS

35. The liturgy of the Mass contains many visual elements, and these should be given great prominence with children. This is especially true of the particular visual elements in the course of the liturgical year, for example, the veneration of the cross, the Easter candle, the lights on the feast of the Presentation of the Lord, and the variety of colours and liturgical ornaments.

In addition to the visual elements that belong to the celebration and to the place of celebration, it is appropriate to introduce other elements which will permit children to perceive visually the great deeds of God in creation and redemption and thus support their prayer. The liturgy should never appear as something dry and merely intellectual.

36. For the same reason the use of pictures prepared by the children themselves may be useful, for example, to illustrate a homily, to give a visual dimension to the intentions of the general intercessions, or to inspire reflection.

SILENCE

37. Even in Masses with children 'silence should be observed at the proper time as a part of the celebration'[32] lest too great a role be given to external action. In their own way children are genuinely capable of reflection. They need, however, a kind of introduction so that they will learn how to reflect within themselves, meditate briefly, or praise God and pray to him in their hearts[33] for example after the homily or after communion.[34]

Besides this, with even greater care than in Masses with adults, the liturgical texts should be spoken intelligibly and unhurriedly, with the necessary pauses.

THE PARTS OF MASS

38. The general structure of the Mass, which 'in some sense consists of two parts, namely, the liturgy of the word and the liturgy of the eucharist,' should always be maintained as should some rites to open and conclude the celebration.[35] Within individual parts of the celebration the adaptations which follow seem necessary if children are truly to experience, in their own way and according to the psychological patterns of childhood, 'the mystery of faith . . . by means of rites and prayers'.[36]

39. Some rites and texts should never be adapted for children lest the difference between Masses with children and the Masses with adults become too great.[37] These are 'the acclamations and the responses of the faithful to the greetings of the priest',[38] the Lord's Prayer, and the trinitarian formula at the end of the blessing with which the priest concludes the Mass. It is urged, moreover, that children should become accustomed to the Nicene Creed little by little, while the use of the Apostles' Creed mentioned in no. 49 is permitted.

a. Introductory Rite

40. The introductory rite of Mass has the purpose 'that the faithful, assembling in unity, should constitute a communion and should prepare themselves properly for hearing the word of God and celebrating the eucharist worthily'.[39] Therefore every effort should be made to create this disposition in the children and to avoid any excess of rites in this part of Mass.

It is sometimes proper to omit one or other element of the introductory rite or perhaps to enlarge one of the elements. There should always be at least some introductory element, which is completed by the opening prayer or collect. In choosing individual elements one should be careful that each one be used at times and that none be entirely neglected.

b. Reading and Explanation of the Word of God

41. Since readings taken from holy scripture constitute 'the principal part of the liturgy of the word',[40] biblical reading should never be omitted even in Masses celebrated with children.

42. With regard to the number of readings on Sundays and feast days, the decrees of the conferences of bishops should be observed. If three or even two readings on Sundays or weekdays can be understood by children only with difficulty, it is permissible to read two or only one of them, but the reading of the gospel should never be omitted.

43. If all the readings assigned to the day seem to be unsuited to the capacity of the children, it is permissible to choose readings or a reading either from the *Lectionary for Mass* or directly from the Bible, taking into account the liturgical seasons. It is urged, moreover, that the individual conferences of bishops prepare lectionaries for Masses with children.

If because of the limited capabilities of the children it seems necessary to omit one or other verse of a biblical reading, this should be done cautiously and in such a way 'that the meaning of the texts or the sense and, as it were, style of the scriptures are not mutilated'.[41]

44. In the choice of readings the criterion to be followed is the quality rather than the quantity of the texts from the scriptures. In itself a shorter reading is not always more suited to children than a lengthy reading. Everything depends upon the spiritual advantage which the reading can offer to children.

45. In the biblical texts 'God speaks to his people . . . and Christ himself is present through his word in the assembly of the faithful'.[42] Paraphrases of scripture should therefore be avoided. On the other hand, the use of translations which may already exist for the catechesis of children and which are accepted by the competent authority is recommended.

46. Verses of psalms, carefully selected in accord with the understanding of children, or singing in the form of psalmody or the alleluia with a simple verse should be sung between the readings. The children should always have a part in this singing, but sometimes a reflective silence may be substituted for the singing.

If only a single reading is chosen, there may be singing after the homily.

47. All the elements which will help to understand the readings should be given great consideration so that the children may make the biblical readings their own and may come more and more to appreciate the value of God's Word.

Among these elements are the introductory comments which may precede the readings [43] and help the children to listen better and more fruitfully, either by explaining the context or by introducing the text itself. In interpreting and illustrating the readings from the scriptures in the Mass on a saint's day, an account of the life of the saint may be given not only in the homily but even before the readings in the form of a commentary.

Where the text of the readings suggest, it may be helpful to have the children read it with parts distributed among them, as is provided for the reading of the Lord's Passion during Holy Week.

48. The homily in which the word of God is unfolded should be

given great prominence in all Masses with children. Sometimes the homily intended for children should become a dialogue with them, unless it is preferred that they should listen in silence.

49. If the profession of faith occurs at the end of the liturgy of the word, the Apostles' Creed may be used with children, especially because it is part of their catechetical formation.

c. Presidential Prayers

50. The priest is permitted to choose from the *Roman Missal* texts of presidential prayers more suited to children, keeping in mind the liturgical season, so that he may truly associate the children with himself.

51. Sometimes this principle of selection is insufficient if the children are to consider the prayers as the expression of their own lives and their own religious experience, since the prayers were composed for adult Christians.[44] In this case the text of prayers of the *Roman Missal* may be adapted to the needs of children, but this should be done in such a way that, preserving the purpose of the prayer and to some extent its substance as well, the priest avoids anything that is foreign to the literary genre of a presidential prayer, such as moral exhortations or a childish manner of speech.

52. The eucharistic prayer is of the greatest importance in the eucharist celebrated with children because it is the high point of the entire celebration.[45] Much depends upon the manner in which the priest proclaims this prayer[46] and in which the children take part by listening and making their acclamations.

The disposition of mind required for this central part of the celebration, the calm and reverence with which everything is done, should make the children as attentive as possible. They should be attentive to the real presence of Christ on the altar under the species of bread and wine, to his offering, to the thanksgiving through him and with him and in him, and to the offering of the Church which is made during the prayer and by which the faithful offer themselves and their lives with Christ to the eternal Father in the Holy Spirit.

For the present, the four eucharistic prayers approved by the supreme authority for Masses with adults are to be employed and kept in liturgical use until the Apostolic See makes other provision for Masses with children.

d. Rites before Communion

53. At the end of the eucharistic prayer, the Lord's Prayer, the breaking of bread, and the invitation to communion should always follow.[47] These elements have the principal significance in the structure of this part of the Mass.

e. Communion and the Following Rites

54. Everything should be done so that the children who are properly disposed and who have already been admitted to the eucharist may go to the holy table calmly and with recollection, so that they may take part fully in the eucharistic mystery. If possible there should be singing, accommodated to the understanding of children, during the communion procession.[48]

The invitation which precedes the final blessing[49] is important in Masses with children. Before they are dismissed they need some repetition and application of what they heard, but this should be done in a very few words. In particular, this is the appropriate time to express the connection between the liturgy and life.

At least sometimes, depending on the liturgical seasons and the different circumstances in the life of the children, the priest should use the richer forms of blessing, but he should always retain the trinitarian formula with the sign of the cross at the end.[50]

---

55. The contents of the directory are intended to help children quickly and joyfully to encounter Christ together in the eucharistic celebration and to stand in the presence of the Father with

him.[51] If they are formed by conscious and active participation in the eucharistic sacrifice and meal, they should learn day by day, at home and away from home, to proclaim Christ to others among their family and among their peers, by living the 'faith, which expresses itself through love' (Galatians 5:6).

This directory was prepared by the Congregation for Divine Worship. On October 22, 1973, the Supreme Pontiff, Paul VI, approved and confirmed it and ordered that it be made public.

From the office of the Congregation for Divine Worship, November 1, 1973, the solemnity of All Saints.

By special mandate of the Supreme Pontiff.

Jean Card. Villot
Secretary of State

+H. Bugnini
Titular Archbishop of Diocletiana
Secretary of the Congregation for Divine Worship

NOTES

1. See Congregation for the Clergy, *Directorium Catechisticum Generale* [=DCG], no. 5: *AAS*, 64 (1972) 101-2.
2. See Vatican Council II, Constitution on the Liturgy, *Sacrosanctum Concilium* [=L], no. 33.
3. See DCG 78: *AAS*, 64 (1972) 146-7.
4. See L 38; also Congregation for Divine Worship, instruction *Actio pastoralis*, May 15, 1969: *AAS*, 61 (1969) 806-11.
5. First Synod of Bishops, Liturgy: *Notitiae*, 3 (1967) 368.
6. See below, nos. 19, 32, 33.
7. See Order of Mass with children who are deafmutes for German-speaking countries, confirmed June 26, 1970, by this congregation (prot. no. 1546/70).
8. See L 14, 19.
9. See DCG 25: *AAS*, 64 (1972) 114.
10. See Vatican Council II, Declaration on Christian Education, *Gravissimum educationis*, no. 2.
11. See *Ibid.*, 3.
12. See DCG 78: *AAS*, 64 (1972) 147.
13. See L 33.
14. See Congregation of Rites, instruction *Eucharisticum mysterium* [=EM], May 25, 1967, no. 14: *AAS* (1967) 550.
15. See DCG 25: *AAS*, 64 (1972) 114.

16. See EM 14: *AAS*, 59 (1967) 550; also DCG 57: *AAS*, 64 (1972) 131.
17. See L 35, 4.
18. See above, no. 3.
19. See L 42, 106.
20. See first Synod of Bishops, Liturgy: *Notitiae*, 3 (1967) 368.
21. See General Instruction of the Roman Missal [=IG], no. 56.
22. See below, no. 37.
23. See IG 11.
24. See L 28.
25. See IG 253.
26. See IG 19.
27. See Congregation of Rites, instruction *Musicam sacram*, March 5, 1967, no. 55: *AAS*, 59 (1967) 316.
28. *Ibid.*, 62: *AAS*, 59 (1967) 318.
29. See above, no. 23.
30. See IG 21.
31. See IG 24.
32. See IG 23.
33. See instruction *Eucharisticum mysterium*, no. 38: *AAS* 59 (1967) 562.
34. See IG 23.
35. See IG 8.
36. See L 48.
37. See above, no. 21.
38. IG 15.
39. IG 24.
40. IG 38.
41. See *Lectionary for Mass*, introduction, no. 7d.
42. IG 33.
43. See IG 11.
44. See Consilium for the Implementation of the Constitution on the Liturgy, Instruction on Translation of Liturgical Texts January 25, 1969, no. 20: *Notitiae*, 5 (1969) 7.
45. See IG 54.
46. See above, nos. 23, 37.
47. See above, no. 23.
48. See instruction *Musicam sacram*, no. 32: *AAS*, 59 (1967) 309.
49. See IG 11.
50. See above, no. 39.
51. See Eucharistic Prayer II.